Latinamericanism after 9/11

D1736904

Post-Contemporary Interventions

SERIES EDITORS: Stanley Fish and Fredric Jameson

Latinamericanism after 9/11

JOHN BEVERLEY

DUKE UNIVERSITY PRESS DURHAM & LONDON 2011

© 2011 Duke University Press
All rights reserved
Printed in the United States of America
on acid-free paper ∞
Designed by Katy Clove
Typeset in Minion by Tseng Information Systems, Inc.
Library of Congress Cataloging-in-Publication Data
appear on the last printed page of this book.

FOR REYNOLDS SMITH

Contents

Introduction

I am not sure exactly when or where the term "Latinamericanism" (or, as it is more usually written, "Latin Americanism") originates. But its current usage is almost certainly a consequence of Edward Said's *Orientalism*, which was originally published in 1978. Alberto Moreiras—whose own book on Latinamericanism, *The Exhaustion of Difference*, I take up in chapter 3—claims that the first use of the term in a sense coincident with Said's comes in two essays by Enrico Mario Santí from the early 1990s, just as the implications of the postcolonial turn, cultural studies, and multicultural identity politics began to percolate into the Latin American field.[1] The first book-length articulation of the term that I am aware of is Román de la Campa's book *Latin Americanism* (1999), which I am indebted to in several ways here—indeed, this book could be considered an updating, or reframing, of some of its major concerns. There (with, however, only a passing reference to Santí) de la Campa describes Latinamericanism as "a community of discourses [about Latin America] that has gained particular force during the past few decades, mainly in the United States, but also beyond."[2] Moreiras himself defines what he calls "Latin Americanist reflection" as "the sum total of academic discourse on Latin America whether carried out in Latin America, the United States, in Europe, or elsewhere."[3]

The word *Latinoamericanismo* appeared prominently in the title of an influential 1998 collection on these issues published in Latin America, *Teorías sin disciplina: Latinoamericanismo, poscolonialidad, y globalización en debate*.[4] In 2002, the Centre for Latin American and Caribbean Studies at the University of Manchester sponsored a conference on "The New Latin Americanism," presumably to distinguish it from a bad, old kind.[5] From the perspective of postcolonial studies Walter Mignolo interrogated both historically and conceptually "the idea of Latin America" in a book of the same title (2004), noting that in its current articulation that idea "is believed to provide a unified front to confront the growing military, economic, and technological invasion coming from the United States. Black and Indigenous communities are fighting for the same cause. . . . ; but they are not doing it in the name of 'Latin' America, since 'Latin' Americans have also been their exploiters" (129–30). Neil Larsen indicted harshly what he calls a "Latin-Americanism without Latin America" based in the U.S. academy and the humanities–cultural studies side of Latin American studies.[6] As if in response to both Mignolo and Larsen, Eduardo Mendieta speaks of "Latinamericanisms," arguing that "Latinamericanism is plural because it has been about how Latin America has been portrayed by at least four major agents of imagination: Latin America itself; the United States, Europe, and, most recently, Latinos. . . . The four types of Latinamericanism register not just a particular chronology but also the shifting of the location, or geopolitical place, of the imaging agent."[7]

These examples could be easily multiplied. They serve only to delimit a certain range of usage of the term in critical discussions of the last fifteen years or so. The latest significant engagement with the idea of Latinamericanism is perhaps Jon Beasley-Murray's *Posthegemony: Political Theory and Latin America* (2010), whose argument I take up in passing at several points in this book (Beasley-Murray was one of the organizers of the conference on the New Latin Americanism mentioned above). I would like to consider in some greater detail here, however, Santí's foundational articulation of the idea of Latinamericanism, which he evokes in rough analogy to Edward Said's concept of Orientalism. Like Orientalism, Santí argues, Latinamericanism produces an "interested *image*" of its object from a distance still defined by an essentially colonial relation:

> By invoking the discourse of Latinamericanism I am merely restating one of the fundamental principles underlying all knowledge regarding Latin America, perhaps regarding the entire so-called third world—namely, the mixture of a Western language and imagination with physical and cultural realities that are only marginally Western. . . . We know many facts about Latin America, but we know little or at least much less about the use

to which the West puts those facts in the construction of a certain interested *image* of Latin America, an image often at odds with the reality from
which those facts are derived. (*Ciphers*, 219)

For Said, Orientalism was basically a form of philology; similarly, for
Santí, philology, as an academic practice involved with the recuperation
or construction of a literary and cultural past, often "national" in character, is the core practice of Latinamericanism. That makes Latinamericanism a discourse formation centered on the humanities, rather than, as
in the dominant paradigms of area studies, the social sciences (though it
does not exclude the social sciences). Santí's claim is that the discourse
of Latinamericanism involves what he calls—borrowing the term from
Geoffrey Hartmann—a "restitutional excess": the recovery of the past in
the name of a present moral, intellectual, and/or ideological imperative.
"Rather than represent the past in its irreducible otherness, philology
translates and reinvents it in the name of mastery of the present Self"
(*Ciphers*, 90). That "mastery of the present Self" is in turn connected to
the assumption that the recovery of a (previously fragmented or mis-
understood) past involves also righting a wrong. That is why it is "restitutional." "A branch of learning with its own specific object, nineteenth-
century philology had an additional ideological mission of its own: to
overcome alienation and restore wholeness and harmony, viewing the
past not merely as an antiquarian object but as broken pieces of a past
whose reintegration into present life would restore a continuity between
past and present" (90). Contemporary Latinamericanism takes the form
of a project of "sympathy"—to use Santí's own word (others might say
"solidarity")[8]—with Latin America (if the project is undertaken from
outside Latin America itself), or of nationalist affirmation (if undertaken
within Latin America). In both cases, the restitution is "excessive" because it seeks to "compensate" in its restoration or creation of the past
some lack, wrong, or alienation that is contained in that past or has been
inflicted on it. Santí writes that, "as a critical practice, restitution is supplementary in character—in compensating for a previous lack it exceeds
rather than simply restores the original" (*Ciphers*, 87).

Said meant by Orientalism the representation by the European academy
and high culture in the nineteenth century (but also before and after that
century) of an Islamic or Asian colonial or semicolonial other. Santí articulates, in his idea of Latinamericanism as a discourse founded on a

perhaps well-meaning but ultimately paternalistic sense of "sympathy," a similar sense of Latinamericanism as an "interested" discourse about Latin America from Europe or the United States. But, for Santí the relation between Latinamericanism and its object is not as one-sided as Orientalism—which, as Said went to some pains to explain, itself involves complex relations of knowledge and authority between metropolitan and local intellectuals. This is for two reasons: first, Latinamericanism is not only the discourse of a metropolitan European or Anglo-American academy *about* a geopolitically peripheral, at one time colonial and now still dependent or subordinate object of study, Latin America; it is also a set of discursive positions and practices internal to Latin America itself, developed in the Latin American public sphere, university knowledge, disciplinary trajectories, art, literature, literary criticism, and cultural debates. Santí's model case of "restitutional excess" is precisely Octavio Paz's famous reading of Sor Juana Inés de la Cruz's renunciation of literature, under pressure from her Church superiors in the late seventeenth century. Santí argues that Paz, in effect, imposes on Sor Juana a framework of choice between authority and the autonomy of the writer and literature that more properly belongs to the debates of the Cold War (for example, in the context of postrevolutionary Cuba) about communism and artistic freedom. In other words, the problem of the "orientalization" of a Latin American subject exists for Santí not only in the philological relation between a metropolitan subject that seeks to "know the other" and a semicolonial or peripheral culture or cultures; it also exists as a problem of "internal colonialism," to use a term that is somewhat out of fashion these days (and that Santí himself does not use): that is, in the relation of the Latin American "lettered city" to its own societies and history.

Where for Santí "restitutional excess" indicates (to use Paul de Man's term) a certain "blindness" in the project of Latinamericanist discourse—whether this is articulated *in* or *about* Latin America—he also understands this excess is also the place where the possible *political* articulation of Latinamericanism, including its implications for the project of the Left (which must take the ideological form of establishing or restoring a reign of justice), reside. And it is that connection between Latinamericanist theory or discourse and liberal or left-wing politics in particular that Santí wants to question. Santí's critique of Latinamericanism as "restitutional excess" is closely connected in particular to the related critique of identity politics in the U.S. academy.[9] For Santí, both Latinamericanism and identity politics could be said to involve a self-satisfied but misguided academic liberalism or "leftism," usually tarred with the charge of "political correctness" (from the right) or of "essentialism" (from the left). The perspective of this book, by contrast, is that there is no clear line of separation between identity politics—and I understand Latinamericanism to be a form of identity politics—and politics. To put this another way, "restitutional excess," which is linked to the affirmation of "identity" (personal, ethnic, racial, class, gender, civic, national, etc.), might be said to be the form of the political as such. So it is not enough simply to point to or "deconstruct" its presence, as Santí does. The question is not whether Latinamericanism is "in" ideology, but rather what kind of ideology is being proposed under that rubric.[10] The chapters in this book have to do with how Latin America itself has become a politically volatile signifier in the new context of globalization, not just a kind of misnomer that never really named its object adequately in the first place. A theme that runs through them is the failure of a certain project of modernity in Latin America, and consequently the need to reimagine Latin American nation-states, societies, cultural identity, and politics at a moment in which not only communism but also a capitalist-neoliberal model of modernization have entered into crisis. At the level of what Walter Benjamin would have called "the experience of the poor," that crisis is registered for me in two recent works of Latin American cultural criticism, Ileana Rodríguez's *Liberalism at Its Limits* and Hermann Herlinghaus's *Violence without Guilt: Ethical Narratives from the Global South*. Both of these texts have to do with the collapse of even imperfect, unequal (but functional) forms of sociality and govermentality in Latin America under the pressure of neoliberal economic restructuring, particularly in the 1990s (it is not by accident that they both center on the question of the U.S.–Mexico border and the violence associated with narcotraffic and the wave of killings of women—the so-called *femicidio*—in Ciudad Juaréz). That collapse forces criticism to think from or about a situation of disaster; but, dialectically as it were, it also raises what Herlinghaus calls "the possibility of criticism in its contamination by the immanence of life itself" (2009, 203). I would hope that this book involves in some small measure that possibility. However, I should also note that my approach here points in a somewhat different direction.

The "text of violence" has become a major trope in Latinamericanist literary and cultural criticism in recent years for reasons that are not hard to comprehend (they are in the latest headlines about the atrocious death toll of the Mexican drug wars or the counterrevolutionary violence in rural Colombia, for example). But I think there is the risk of representing Latin America as essentially violent and ungovernable. I want to indicate here also what seems to me promising or hopeful in the immediate horizon of Latin America's becoming. In particular, I am trying to register what I think is a shift in circumstances — it might be useful to characterize it as postneoliberal — that may warrant new theoretical and critical approaches. This is in part what I mean by a Latinamericanism that is *after* 9/11. Let me explain.

Why, if my point is to write about something that has to do with Latin America, do I choose as a title *Latinamericanism after 9/11* (9/11 being an event particular to the United States), rather than something like *Latinamericanism and the Bicentennial*, invoking thus the anniversary of the first formal declarations of independence from Spain of different regions of Latin America in 1810? It is a commonplace that everyone had the thought on 9/11 that things would never be the same again. By "after 9/11," then, I mean to indicate the sea change in everything from geopolitics to the individual psyche that occurs in the wake of the terrorist attacks on that date. In terms of the relation between the United States and Latin America in particular, 9/11 could be said to inaugurate a double movement that comes not only "after" but also to some extent *because of* the effects of 9/11 and its aftermath. Before 9/11, and especially during the Clinton presidency in the 1990s, geopolitically the United States and the neoliberal assumptions of the so-called Washington consensus were hegemonic in every sphere of Latin American life. After 9/11, that hegemony begins to fade. The United States turns increasingly in a right-wing direction, leading to, externally, the invasions of Iraq and Afghanistan and the War on Terror, and, internally, the process of deregulation that culminated in the economic crisis of 2009. A significant part of Latin America, on the other hand, begins to shift away from identification with U.S. power post-9/11. The strong disinclination of Latin American governments (with one or two exceptions) to send troops to the Coalition of the Willing in Iraq and Afghanistan marks one of the first breaks since the 1970s from the model of regional economic and geopolitical integration under U.S. auspices represented by NAFTA and the Washington consensus.

More specifically, however, what the phrase "after 9/11" is meant to in-

6

voke is the appearance in the last decade or so of a series of new governments of the Left in Latin America of a very varied character: the "Pink Tide" or *marea rosada* that has engulfed the whole continent. The roots of the marea rosada are in the bloody urban upheaval that took place in Venezuela on February 27, 1989 (the "Caracazo"), and the subsequent emergence of Hugo Chávez as a political leader, then the sharp economic crises in the late 1990s and early years of the new century, including notably the Brazilian devaluation of 1999 and the economic collapses of Ecuador in 1999–2000 and of Argentina in 2001. In electoral terms, the first instance of the marea rosada is the Chávez government of 1998. But as a general movement or trend, it certainly comes into its own in the years after 9/11, when the United States turned its attention away from Latin America, and Latin American states began to shift away from an identification with both the geopolitical and economic frameworks of the Washington consensus.

Whatever its eventual outcome (does it herald a more general and deeper radicalization, or is it forced by its own self-imposed reformism to be a kind of Latin American capitalism with a human face?), the marea rosada has the character of what the French philosopher Alain Badiou calls an "event": that is, something unexpected, unpredicted, radically contingent and overdetermined, but which, in that very contingency and overdetermination, opens up a new, unforeseen, and unforeseeable series of possibilities and determinations. Let me be clear that this is not a book about the marea rosada as such. It is however a book founded on the assumption that the marea rosada—whatever its outcome—has shifted the grounds of Latinamericanist thinking in a significant way. It has done so, in the first place, by giving a new ideological and geopolitical force to the idea of Latin America itself.

The governments of the marea rosada are of a very heterogeneous character, but in spite of their ideological and at times economic points of difference and conflict, they share a common political identity as governments of the Left (they are perhaps more accurately center-left governments, but the shift in what the idea of "Left" means is itself part of the dynamic of the marea rosada),[11] and a project (postneoliberal regional economic cooperation and affirmation). At moments of crisis—for example, the attempted putsch by reactionary groups in the province of Santa Cruz in Bolivia in 2008—they support each other, often via newly created regional deliberative bodies like UNASUR (the Unión de Naciones

Suramericanas) or the ALBA (Alianza Bolivariana para los Pueblos de Nuestra América). Though sometimes they have roots in popular insurrections, such as the Caracazo in Venezuela or the indigenous blockades in Ecuador and Bolivia, they work effectively and comfortably within the framework of constitutional democracy and electoral politics, which they accept. Where existing constitutional provisions represent an impediment to their political and social projects, they tend to avail themselves of the device of the constitutional referendum, with, in general, success. They see the horizon of socialism as essentially a *democratic* one, and their aim is to deepen democratic participation among sectors of the population marginalized or excluded from formal political dialogue.

I do not wish to minimize the fact that the marea rosada involves many ambiguities, contradictions, and uncertainties. Its very nature seems to make it open to both ideological and strategic pluralism. Like any human enterprise it is subject to failure or to the perversion of its goals. Indeed recent events, like the coup in Honduras, the attempted coup in Ecuador, or the election of right-wing candidates in Chile and Colombia, suggest that the "tide" may in fact be ebbing, and that a reactionary axis is beginning to take shape in Latin America. And many readers will find the marea rosada altogether too "reformist" or "populist" for their taste in any case.[12]

Nevertheless, it seems worth remarking that today, some twenty years after the collapse of the Soviet Union and "actually existing socialism," a majority of the population of Latin America lives under democratically elected governments that identify themselves as "socialist" in one way or another. To put this another way, the only place in the world today where socialism, even as a rhetorical possibility, is on the agenda is Latin America. What "socialism" means in this case is subject to debate, but that of course was true in the cases of both communism and European social democracy too.

The events of 9/11 followed by only days the meeting of the Latin American Studies Association in Washington, D.C., in which the disbanding of the Latin American Subaltern Studies Group was announced publicly (those participants in the conference who stayed on in Washington for a day or two afterward would have witnessed the attack on the Pentagon). My own work up to that point was tied closely to subaltern studies. This book is not only "after 9/11," then, it is also in some ways postsubalternist. This is indicated particularly by the attention given here to the question of the state. The paradigm implicit in subaltern studies (and in postmod-

8

ernist social theory in general) was that of the separation of the state and the subaltern. The intention was to recognize and support both previously existing and newly emergent forms of resistance that did not pass through conventional historical narratives of state formation and statist forms of citizenship and political or social participation. We are now confronted paradoxically in some ways by the success of a series of political initiatives in Latin America that, speaking very broadly, corresponded to the concerns of subaltern studies. In a situation where, as is the case of several governments of the marea rosada, social movements from the popular-subaltern sectors of society have "become the state," to borrow a phrase from Ernesto Laclau, or are bidding to do so, a new way of thinking the relationship between the state and society has become necessary.

The project of Latin American subaltern studies developed in a close, one might say "fraternal" relation with deconstruction—in fact, we were sometimes taken to task for this by historians such as Florencia Mallon. We wanted to say "from the left," so to speak, the same thing that Santí was saying "from the right": that a certain cultural discourse of Latin American modernity and identity had reached, with the waning of the revolutionary impulse of the 1960s and 1970s, a kind of limit. In assembling the material for this book, however, I have become aware that this identification of subalternism, leftism, and deconstruction has become problematic for me. My sense is that deconstruction is yielding diminishing and politically ambiguous returns, and that this has something to do with the way in which both 9/11 and the emergence of the marea rosada have shifted the grounds of theory and criticism in our time.

So what? Is there in any case any really meaningful connection between the discourses of academic Latinamericanism and politics on the ground? The answer I offer in these chapters is not much (and it is important to understand why that is the case), but some, enough to make a difference sometimes. The golden age of academic theory is rapidly fading, if not already past. So much so, that what is presented here may simply be the ashes of a fire that has already been extinguished. Moreover, as Santí asks, hasn't all the fuss about theory—even in nominally postcolonial forms—been mainly a case of U.S. and European intellectuals (or Latin American intellectuals in the U.S. or European academy) speaking to each other *about* Latin America?

Let me offer in response to both of these issues—that is, the question of "bringing the state back in," as the current phrase has it, and the question of the waning of theory (or its impertinence with respect to Latin America)—a small, and probably inadequate anecdote. It concerns the current vice president of Bolivia, Álvaro García Linera. In the 1990s García Linera was associated with an academic collective in Bolivia called Comuna, which resembled in some ways both the South Asian and the Latin American Subaltern Studies Groups. It was in part out of the work of Comuna that key features of the ideological and political project of the MAS (Movimiento al Socialismo) evolved, particularly around the question of how to articulate hegemonically the heterogeneous or "motley" (*abigarrado*), multicultural character of the Bolivian popular sectors.[13] Two Bolivian academics who were close to but not formally part of Comuna, Silvia Rivera Cusicangui and Rossana Barragán, translated and published in Bolivia a selection of texts by the South Asian group, including Gayatri Spivak's well-known essay "Deconstructing Historiography."[14] They saw this gesture as involving a "South-South" dialogue that explicitly cut out U.S.-based Latinamericanism as an interlocutor. I think it is fair to assume that García Linera probably read this collection or parts of it, and almost certainly knew of it. If that is true, then subaltern studies itself has become—oxymoronically—part of the state.

There is no clear lesson here: Comuna itself recently split, and there has been a parallel polarization within the MAS government around the role of García Linera. But my anecdote does suggest that theory can have consequences. Those consequences can be enabling for political practice: as in the case of Comuna and García Linera, one can claim that the interaction between theory and Latinamericanism "opens up" new spaces and new forms for the articulation of the Left that were not available in the previous period of radicalization in the 1960s and 1970s. On the other hand, theory that has become outdated or missed its mark, as I have come to think is the case with deconstruction, can also lead to errors or impasses in political practice.

Because it is also part of what "after 9/11" encompasses, let me remark briefly on the relationship between the United States and Latin America—a repeated concern in these chapters. President Obama promised what he called a New Partnership with Latin America, a sort of neoliberalized version of the Good Neighbor Policy. Some—I include myself—may have even imagined for a moment that the election of Obama and the extent of the economic crisis heralded a political shift in the United States itself that would be syntonic in some ways with the marea rosada. But, with the exception of some very welcome new initiatives (in the matter of U.S.-Cuban relations, for example), there is more continuity than change in Obama's Latin American policy. Its ultimate goal appears to be to continue to affirm or reaffirm U.S. regional hegemony. If this reading is correct, unless there is a significant shift of direction, the Obama administration will seek, rather than a relation of mutual sympathy with the marea rosada, a strategy to limit it within a framework acceptable to established U.S. interests. Hugo Chávez has remarked that Obama remains a "prisoner of empire." A harsh judgment, but one that is hard to avoid, however much one wishes Obama well.

Obama and his people have been guided in their approach to Latin America by what has come to be known as the doctrine of the "two Lefts." As enunciated by Jorge Castañeda in an influential article in *Foreign Affairs*, the resurgent Latin American Left is seen as divided between "a modern, democratic, globalized, and market-friendly left" and "a retrograde, populist, authoritarian, statist, and anti-American left."[15] The task of U.S. policy toward Latin America should be to encourage the first and discourage the second. (It could be argued from that premise, for example, that what made the coup in Honduras finally acceptable to the Obama administration was that it was directed against a president, Zelaya, who was seen as having close ties with Chávez. Zelaya, in other words, belonged to or was seen as moving in the direction of the "retrograde Left"; if he had been of the "moderate Left," on the other hand, like the former president of Chile, Michelle Bachelet, the coup would not have been tolerated.)

There are indeed many, and often deep, differences among the new governments of the marea rosada in Latin America, but they do not resolve themselves into Castañeda's neat dichotomy, which has at best the character of a self-fulfilling prophecy. Even if there were something more to the dichotomy than simple wishful thinking, should the Obama administration in any case commit itself to a policy that puts it on a collision course with democratically elected governments in Brazil, Bolivia, Venezuela, Ecuador, Paraguay, Argentina, El Salvador, Uruguay, Guatemala, and Nicaragua? There are no doubt authoritarian "tendencies" among Chávez and perhaps other leaders of the marea rosada, but on the whole the Tide has been a democratic one, whereas the efforts to stem it—like the failed coup against Chávez, or the coup against Zelaya in Honduras and the attempted putsch in Santa Cruz, or the militarization of the Colombian countryside—have not been.

Behind the retrograde/modern, hard/soft Left dichotomy is a premise that the "market-friendly" good guys on the Left are those still willing to work within a framework conforming to the existing structure of international trade and markets, whereas the bad guys question that framework and are looking for ways to get out of it (by, for example, repudiating foreign debt). The most expansive and influential presentation of this argument, which is the corollary in the field of political economy of the doctrine of the "two Lefts," is Michael Reid's *Forgotten Continent*, which centers on "the battle for Latin America's soul" supposedly being waged today, Reid believes, largely out of sight of the rest of the world, because Latin America dropped off the geopolitical screen after the end of the Cold War and the shift of U.S. policy in particular toward the Middle East after 9/11 (Reid is the Latin American correspondent for *The Economist*). It is a battle between the "democratic reformism" exemplified by countries such as Chile or Brazil and a state-driven "populist autocracy" represented by Chávez or Morales. There remain great problems in Latin American societies, above all poverty and inequality, Reid admits. But these will be best addressed by a process of institutional reform within the free market and existing political structures, rather than by a return to the state-centered recipes of the past. In particular, the populist edge of the marea rosada represents a politically dangerous and in economic terms potentially disastrous trend, which must be contained and reversed. Reid's conclusion is that Latin America should essentially return to a new, softer version of the Washington consensus, now modified in the direction of providing greater financial stability and addressing pressing social demands.

But that way of formulating the choice that faces Latin America, like Castañeda's idea of the "two Lefts," has the character of a self-fulfilling prophecy. Reid questions this assumption, but most people think that the resurgence of the Latin American Left may be attributed largely if not exclusively to the enormous social problems created by the neoliberal economic policies dominant during the 1980s and 1990s, problems that were also behind the waves of immigration to the United States, and within Latin America itself, during those years. (Another way to put this is that the crisis of the neoliberal model was experienced in Latin America about a decade or so before it was felt in the United States and Europe in 2009, especially in the economic collapses of 1999–2002.) The strategies for responding to these problems may differ from country to country, depending on degree of industrialization, energy requirements, local politi-cal considerations, relations with external markets, trends in prices of raw materials, and the like, but there is no doubt that *all* the new governments of the marea rosada, of whatever character, understand the need to move beyond the Washington consensus.[16]

The book that, from the Latin American side of things, could be said to coincide in some ways with Castañeda's idea of a U.S. foreign policy that favors the moderate Left and challenges the "populist" Left and with Reid's prescription for a return to the Washington consensus, is Jorge Volpi's *El insomnio de Bolívar*, a kind of panorama of the situation of Latin America on the eve of the Bicentennial of its independence.[17] Volpi is a talented writer, and he offers a fresh, humorous, sharp-eyed, but also, it needs to be said, deeply reactionary view of Latin America today, of the marea rosada in particular, and of the possibility of anything like an affirmative Latin-americanism, whether this is populist-nationalist or the good-hearted but paternalistic liberalism of "sympathy" critiqued by Santí. He addresses himself in particular to the new, post-leftist generation (his own) of the educated middle class that has come of age in Latin America in or since the 1990s and that is anxious to be rid of what might be called the "Oedi-pal" burden of both an immediate and a deep Latin American histori-cal past, and the set of literary and cultural markers associated with that past, including among other things the "magic realism" of the novels of the Latin American Boom. One has the sense that Volpi is bidding to be something like the Latin American Flaubert.[18]

His book centers on a strikingly provocative question in that regard:

> Preguntémonos entonces, otra vez, ¿qué compartimos, en exclusiva, los latinoamericanos? ¿Lo mismo de siempre: la lengua, las tradiciones cató-licas, el derecho romano, unas cuantas costumbres de incierto origen indí-gena o africano y el recelo, ahora transformado en chistes y gracejadas, hacia España y los Estados Unidos? ¿Es todo? ¿Después de dos siglos de vida independiente eso es todo? ¿De verdad? (85)

> [Let us ask ourselves, then, once again, what do we Latin Americans share in particular? The same things as always: the language, Catholic traditions, Roman Law, a few customs of uncertain indigenous or African origin, and the resentment, now transformed into jokes and witticisms, of Spain and the United States? Is that all? After two centuries of independence is that all? Truly all?]

The answer Volpi offers is equally striking: "Quizá la única manera de llevar a cabo el sueño de Bolívar sea dejando de lado a América Latina" (148) [Perhaps the only way to realize Bolívar's dream is to abandon Latin America]. In a comic-prophetic "Cronología del futuro" at the end of his book, Volpi envisions the following sequence of events: the disappearance of his own country, Mexico, via its incorporation into the United States; then the division of the continent in two more or less cohesive regions, North and South America, with Central America and the Caribbean negotiating between them; in 2035 the creation of an "Alliance of the South" and in 2044 of a "North American Union"; war between the two entities in 2049; a gradual period of détente, leading to the formal proclamation in 2098 of something called los Estados Unidos de las Américas, the United States of the Americas; a subsequent period of civic turmoil similar to that which preceded the ratification of the Constitution in the United States; then, finally, in 2110, the emergence de facto of the new entity. That chronology is in fact the scenario of Bolívar's last *insomnio*; with its completion, he can finally sleep: "Una América unida, menudo disparate. Sabe que el fin está cerca y de pronto se siente tranquilo, en paz. Casi sonríe mientras su semblante se llena de luz. Al fin podrá dormir" (259) [A single, united America: what a crazy idea. He knows that the end is near and suddenly he feels tranquil, at peace. He almost smiles as his face fills with light. Finally he can sleep].

As for the marea rosada in particular, it is an illusion:

El anunciado—y para muchos temido—despertar de la izquierda en América Latina es un espejismo o un malentendido. Cada país mantiene una dinámica propia y, más allá de la contaminación entre unos gobiernos y otros—y el errático internacionalismo de Chávez—, el triunfo o el avance de los partidos o líderes de la izquierda obedecen más a tensiones sociales y económicas internas que a una suerte de epidemia regional. . . . No existe, para decirlo llanamente *una* izquierda latinoamericana. (133–34, 135)

[The announcement—feared by many—of the awakening of the Left in Latin America is an illusion or a misunderstanding. Each country has its own dynamic and, beyond the contamination between one government and another—and the erratic internationalism of Chávez—the triumph or the advance of parties or leaders of the Left obeys more internal social and economic tensions than a sort of regional epidemic. There does not exist in fact *a* Latin American Left.]

There is in Volpi's proposal an understandable desire on the part of a younger generation in Latin America to be rid of the weight of ossified discourses and expectations, but also something old and not all that unfamiliar after all. I refer to the "annexationist" strain in certain strands of nineteenth-century Latin American liberalism that saw integration with the United States as the best course for the future. There are unexpected points of coincidence between my argument and his (for example, we both believe the war against drugs should be ended and drug use decriminalized), but I think it would be fair to say that *El insomnio de Bolívar* represents the most explicit alternative to the "Latinamericanism" or "Latinamericanisms" that are in play, often in debate with one another, in the pages of this book. What Volpi means by a "regional epidemic" is essentially what I mean by "Latinamericanism after 9/11," that is, the possibility of articulating together new positions in academic theory with new possibilities for political and social change. However, *El insomnio de Bolívar* is also a text *of* Latinamericanism, just as much as, say, *La unidad latinoamericana*, a recent collection of the speeches of Hugo Chávez, who is, it goes without saying, the nemesis of everything Volpi stands for. Each text is marked from opposing sides of the Latin American political and social divide by its own version of "restitutional excess."

Volpi raises the question of the massive waves of Latin American immigration to United States, which implies for him that his own country, Mexico, is now being absorbed de facto into the United States and Canada. But there is the other side of that: that is, what is happening when, with a Hispanic population currently estimated at forty-five million and rapidly growing, the United States is on the road to becoming in the next ten years or so, after Mexico, the second largest nation of the Spanish-speaking world, surpassing Spain itself in that regard. It is not surprising that in his final book *Who Are We?*, Samuel Huntington saw the "clash of civilizations" as *internal* to the United States, arguing that Hispanic immigration, rather than radical Islam, would be the greatest threat to the future of the United States as a nation-state. By the same token, many Latin American intellectuals have tended to see the growing demographic presence of immigrants from Latin America in the United States and the corresponding rise of new forms of Latino culture (and speech) as a question of immigrant assimilation and acculturation to U.S. norms, rather than as an extension of the possibility of Latin America itself. Like Huntington, but from the other side, they are concerned to police the border between North and South. But the reality on the ground is that the border is an increasingly anachronistic and violent fiction. Some ten to twelve million Hispanics in the United States are undocumented immigrants. The question of what to do with them is the most intractable issue in U.S. politics today. But they are not going to go away, nor can they be repatriated en masse. Nor can the United States effectively check further immigration, even with very heavy policing such as that portended by the new measures adopted by the state of Arizona. Nor can the Hispanic population, both citizens and permanent residents and the undocumented, be integrated via the previously powerful forces of immigrant acculturation. Indeed, Alejandro Portes and Alex Stepik, writing about Miami, speak of Hispanic immigration and demographic growth as producing an "acculturation in reverse."[19]

It follows then that, obliged by the demographic reality of its actual population, the United States will have to become as a nation something other than it is (or imagines itself to be) today, something perhaps not all that different from what the Bolivians had in mind when in the 2009 constitutional referendum they redefined Bolivia as a plurinational state, *un Estado Plurinacional*. This is a way of saying that there is not a clear line of distinction between a new Latinamericanism and a new Americanism, and therefore that the issues discussed here also pertain in some ways to the possibility of creating a new discourse of the Left in the United States.

CHAPTER ONE

Latinamericanism after 9/11

Let me begin by recalling the well-known passage in *The Philosophy of History* where Hegel, writing in 1822, anticipates the future of the United States:

> Had the woods of Germany been in existence, the French Revolution would not have occurred. North America will be comparable with Europe only after the immeasurable space which that country presents to its inhabitants shall have been occupied, and the members of the political body shall have begun to be pressed back on each other. North America is still in the condition of having land to begin to cultivate. Only when, as in Europe, the direct increase of agriculture is checked, will the inhabitants, instead of pressing outwards to occupy the fields, press inwards on each other . . . and so form a compact system of civil society, and require an organized state. . . . America is therefore the land of the future, where, in the ages that lie before us, the burden of the World's History shall reveal itself — perhaps in a contest between North and South America. It is a land of desire for all those who are weary of the historical lumber-room of old Europe.[1]

Following Hegel, should we believe that the future of Latin America will necessarily involve a conflict with the United States "in the ages that lie before us?" I think that the answer is yes. If September 11, 1973, marked the beginning of a long period of conservative restoration in the Americas, including the United States, it seems clear, as I suggested in my introduction, that Latin America has entered a new period in the aftermath of September 11, 2001, 9/11. If the tonic of the previous period was the integration of Latin America with the United States under the banner of neoliberalism—the idea of the so-called Washington consensus—the new period portends an increasing confrontation between Latin America and North American hegemony, in several areas: cultural, economic, and, perhaps, military too.[2]

That prospect brings to mind Samuel Huntington's idea of the "clash of civilizations."[3] Huntington suggests that new forms of conflict in the world after the Cold War would no longer be structured along the bipolar model of communism versus capitalism, but rather would crystallize along heterogeneous "fault lines" of ethnic, cultural, linguistic, and religious differences, which generate potentially antagonistic geopolitical blocs: the United States–United Kingdom–British Commonwealth; Europe (a Europe divided between east and west, "new" and "old"); East Asia ("Confucian") and the Indian subcontinent ("Hindu"); sub-Saharan Africa; and the Islamic world in all of its extension and internal complexity, stretching across Asia, Africa, and into Europe and the Americas. In Huntington's taxonomy, the nations of Latin America and the Caribbean are, like Turkey or Russia with respect to Europe, "torn countries." Will they define their future by a symbiotic and dependent relationship with the cultural and economic hegemony of the United States, or can they develop, individually or collectively, as a region or "civilization," their own projects in competition with or in the place of that hegemony?[4]

But, one might ask, what is the point of talking about Latin America as a "civilization," or, for that matter, about *Latin* America, which is a doubly colonial double misnomer (first, for the name of the Italian navigator, and second, for the idea of "Latinity" promulgated by the French Foreign Office in the nineteenth century to try to displace U.S. and British hegemony)?[5] Shouldn't we be concerned instead with marking the limits of intelligibility of concepts such as "civilization" or "nation?"

My question, however, is a different one. From a sense precisely of these limits, in which the authority of concepts of nation, identity, or civilization—perhaps even of "culture" itself—is brought into question, what would be the form of a *new* Latinamericanism, capable of confronting U.S. hegemony and expressing an alternative future for the peoples of the Americas? For Hegel, what delayed the coming to fruition of the United States as a nation was the continental frontier, because the expansion of the frontier did not allow the formation of a coherent civil society among its inhabitants. What has delayed, not the confrontation between Latin

America and the United States (because this already has a history of more than three hundred years—the "immense space" that Hegel refers to was precisely one of its dimensions), but rather the successful affirmation of Latin America in that confrontation, has been the continuation in Latin America of elements from its colonial past, combined with a postcolonial model, the "liberal" nationalism of the new republics in the nineteenth century, which created stunted, dependent economies, and marginalized or repressed broad sectors of the continent's peoples and cultures.

One of the signs—perhaps minor in the scheme of things, but nevertheless symptomatic—of polarization between the United States and Latin America was the rejection or questioning by significant sectors of the Latin American intelligentsia of trends in academic "theory" such as postmodernism, cultural studies, postcolonial and subaltern studies, and U.S.-style multiculturalism. The fusion of "theory" and Latin American studies collectively constitutes what is usually meant by Latinamericanism, which is seen from the perspective of Latin America itself as a discourse formation involving at best an attempt to impose agendas from the U.S. academy and civil society onto Latin American contexts where they do not fit well, and at worst an outright colonization of Latin American intellectual agendas by forms of theory elaborated in the North American and Ibero-European academy and area studies.[6]

This position can be defined as neo-Arielist, for its opposition to an intellectual "fashion" identified with the United States—Mabel Moraña spoke famously of "el *boom* del subalterno"[7]—and its affirmation, in response, of the authority of a prior and ongoing tradition of Latin American literary, cultural, and theoretical work. (The reference is, of course, to José Enrique Rodó's *Ariel*, written at the end of the nineteenth century, when the United States begins to loom large in the affairs of Latin America, where Rodó famously counterposes the figure of Ariel in Shakespeare's *Tempest*, the poet or "spirit of the air," as representing Latin American civilization, to the "deformed" Caliban, as representing the vulgarity and utilitarianism of U.S. commercial society.) But neo-Arielism is also a form of Latinamericanism, a "Latin American Latinamericanism," to borrow a phrase from Alberto Moreiras. I will return to that question more extensively in chapter 4. Let me just sketch briefly the argument I develop there. The problem with neo-Arielism as a form of Latinamericanism, it seems to me, is not that it is nationalist or anti-Yankee, but rather that it is not so in a sufficiently effective way. It affirms the value of the "Latin American" against the United States, of Spanish or Portuguese against English, and of writing *from* rather than *about* Latin America (I allude here as elsewhere in these essays to Nelly Richard's distinction of critical theory written "desde" rather than "sobre Latinoamérica"). But it is not now (nor was it when Rodó wrote *Ariel*) an adequate response to U.S. cultural and economic hegemony. This is because its vision of the natural resources and human possibilities of Latin America is too limited, stunted by its own dependence on a colonial genealogy it has been unable to overcome. It shares this limitation with dependency theory, for which it serves, in some ways, as a cultural correlative. It is not able to represent and group together all the heterogeneous and multifaceted elements that actually make up the nation; it does not have the capacity to produce a genuinely "national-popular" appeal, to recall Gramsci's concept. But, beyond the nation, it also cannot articulate in a radically new way Latin America as a "civilization," in the sense that Huntington gives to this concept, under conditions of globalization. It produces and reproduces a perpetual division between the culture of the intelligentsia and elites—including liberal or leftist intellectuals—and the popular sectors. It represents, more than the conditions of impoverishment, inequality, and resistance of the popular sectors, the anxiety of intellectuals of bourgeois or middle-class background, generally ethnically European or mestizo, who are threatened with being pushed off the stage of history by, on the one hand, neoliberalism and globalization and, on the other, a heterogeneous and multiform proletarian/popular subject on whose behalf they had pretended to speak.

In this sense, the neo-Arielist position, which continues to be dominant among the cultural and intellectual elites of Latin America, and in the humanities side of the Latin American academy in particular, reproduces the constitutive anxiety of the initial Arielism of Rodó and the *modernistas*, who manifested a deep, visceral anti–North Americanism together with a disdain for (or fear of) the masses (including the new immigrant population) and mass democracy. It rests on an overestimation, colonial in origin, of the authority of written literature and the literary essay and an essentially Eurocentric sense of the cultural canon and aesthetic "value." While it often tends to celebrate "cultural criticism" over "cultural studies," which is seen as a U.S. phenomenon, it has shown itself curiously incapable of critiquing its own limitations.[8] Instead, it has to defend and reterritorialize these limitations in order to present itself as an

alternative to what it sees as "metropolitan" or "populist" academic fash-
ions such as cultural studies. In this sense, although it accuses "studies" of
orientalizing the Latin American subject, the neo-Arielist position cannot
or does not want to see adequately the orientalization that has operated,
and still operates, within the Latin American "lettered city," of which it
remains an integral part. (The history of Latin American literature could
be written in some ways as the history of the discursive orientalization by
Latin American literary intellectuals of large sectors of the population of
Latin America.)

The underlying problem has to do with the relation between democracy and cultural identity. What is it that we understand a democratic
and egalitarian society to be? Those of us who work in the field of Latin
American cultural studies are in one way or another conscious that we
face a paradox in what we do. Beyond our differences, we share a desire
for cultural democratization and social justice. That desire comes from
our connection with an earlier project of the Left in both the United States
and Latin America, which wanted to install new forms of politics, ones
that were thought to be more capable of representing the popular sectors.
Perhaps this aspiration has itself become problematic for some. But if we
still accept the principles of cultural democratization and egalitarianism
as a goal, today we find ourselves in a situation in which what we do can
be complicit with precisely that which we want to resist: the deconstructive force of the market and neoliberal ideology. It was Néstor García
Canclini who articulated this paradox the most lucidly, without finding,
in my opinion, a way out of it, beyond the slogan — valid but limited — "el
consumo sirve para pensar," consumer choice is a way of thinking.[9]

I think that the task that faces the Latinamericanist project today has
to begin with the recognition that globalization and neoliberal political
economy have done, more effectively than ourselves, the work of cultural
democratization and dehierarchization. This explains in part why neoliberalism — in spite of its origins in extreme counterrevolutionary violence — became an ideology in which some sectors of subaltern classes
or groups could also see possibilities for themselves. To use a distinction
made by Ranajit Guha, unlike British colonial rule in India, neoliberalism has been not only a *dominant* but also a *hegemonic* ideology in Latin
America. But that hegemony is beginning to crumble.

If I am correct in this prognostication, the neo-Arielist project of finding refuge from the disaggregating forces of globalization and neoliberal

"structural adjustment" in a Borgesian reterritorialization of the figure of the critical intellectual, the literary canon, and the notion of aesthetic as opposed to practical reason shows itself as a position that is too defensive and that risks (as I will argue in chapter 5) lending itself to a neoconservative turn, antineoliberal but also suspicious of new forms of agency emerging from the social movements and corresponding new forms of radical or "populist" politics. The crisis of the Latin American Left that coincided with, or led to, neoliberal hegemony in the 1970s and 1980s did not result from a scarcity of brilliant aesthetic, political, economic, historiographic, or pedagogical models of what Latin America has been or could be, but rather from just the opposite: the excessive presence of the intellectual class and its own values and ambitions in the formulation of models of identity, governability, and development.

What neoliberal theory celebrates is the possibility of a heterogeneity of social actors allowed by market society—a play of differences that is not subject, in principle, to the dialectic of the master and the slave, because according to the calculus of rational choice, individuals try to maximize their advantages and minimize their disadvantage in the marketplace, without obliging others to give up their interests, and without necessarily paying attention to the values of both traditional and modern intellectuals. By contrast, in some of its best known variants—for example, the ideal of the New Man championed by Che Guevara—the Left put forward a normative and voluntarist model of what the Latin American popular-democratic subject *should be*. If the goal of this insistence was to produce a properly socialist modernity, a more complete modernity than the bourgeois "peripheral" modernity inhibited and deformed by neocolonialism and dependent capitalism, then we would have to recognize that the project of the Left in Latin America, including the Cuban Revolution, substituted for socialism as such—that is, a state and society led by and for the popular classes—a development-oriented model of economic and cultural modernization carried out in the name of the "people," but put forward on the whole by technocrats and intellectuals.[10]

If the conflict between capitalism and socialism in the Cold War was essentially a struggle to see which of the two systems could better produce modernity, then history has rendered its verdict on that score: capitalism. To limit the possibilities of socialism simply to the fight to achieve a more complete modernity is to condemn the Left, or what remains of it, to failure in advance. The possibility of fashioning a new Latinamericanism capable of both inspiring and nourishing itself from new forms of political and social practice "from below," so to speak, depends on the possibility of imagining a vision of the socialist project that is not tied to the teleology of modernity, but that, on the other hand, does not imply a simple renunciation of modernity either. That task would involve recovering for the discourse of the Left the space of cultural dehierarchization ceded to the market and to neoliberalism, and now claimed by postmodernist intellectuals in Latin America like Jorge Volpi.

The challenge of ideological articulation that this presupposes is to link together three different, but ultimately related processes: (1) cultural democratization—the opening toward difference and toward new forms of freedom and personal identity; (2) the affirmation of the distinctness of Latin America as a "civilization" in the face of North American and European domination, without falling back on the exhausted formulas of a complacent creole-mestizo nationalism; (3) the necessity of displacing in the near or distant future, if not capitalism as such, then at least its economic hegemony and its bureaucratic rationality. As I will argue in chapter 4, in order to meet this challenge, it seems to me that the posture represented by the different forms of "studies" (cultural, subaltern, women's, ethnic, queer, postcolonial, multicultural, etc.), is more useful in the long run than the neo-Arielist posture that seems on the surface to be more immediately nationalist. This is because the possible (or inevitable) confrontation of Latin America with the United States requires a *redefinition* of the Latin American nation: not only of what it has been, but also of what it might and should be. This redefinition cannot come principally from the economic and cultural elites, nor from the tradition of the Latin American "lettered city," nor, on the whole, from the remnants of the historical Left, because in essence all these sectors remain anchored to the project of modernity that has produced and maintains Latin America as it is today. It requires, instead, a political and cultural intentionality that arises from "others." This realization lay behind the idea—today perhaps too generalized and for that reason in danger of being neutralized—of the subaltern and subaltern studies.

What would be the elements of a Latinamericanism articulated "from" the subaltern? It is beyond my competence to answer this question, and the point of a neo-Arielism would be to question my authority to do so. But some of those elements are already in evidence with the emergence of the governments of the marea rosada (and beyond them). They would include a recognition of the theoretical originality produced by the Latin American social movements, which have been not only "objects" of theory but also its creators, in ways that sometimes bypass or contest the agency of traditional intellectuals; the "Bolivarian" affirmation of forms of territoriality that go beyond the nation-state (the historical nation is like a beloved home, which we feel we must defend, but also which we find too confining); the consequent redefinition of Latin America itself (including the Hispanic populations of the United States) as a "multinational state";[11] a recognition of the continuing importance economically (and culturally) for Latin America of agriculture and of a peasantry and rural population increasingly threatened by globalization;[12] the survival and demographic recovery of the indigenous peoples of the continent with their own languages, cultures, and economies, not just as semiautonomous groups within existing nation-states, but rather as constitutive elements of the identity of those nations and of Latin America itself; the continuing struggle against racism in all of its forms, and for the complete equality of the Afro-Latino, mulatto, and mestizo populations;[13] the struggles of women and sexual minorities against misogyny, homophobia, and machismo, and in favor of not only legal but also substantive gender equality; workers' struggles in both the countryside and the cities, in which they confront increasingly brutal capitalist regimes, to take control of the forces of production not only in their own name as a class, but also in the collective interest of society as a whole; and the mobilization and integration of that immense sector of the population of Latin America that lives in barrios, favelas, slums, and shantytowns, and waits, generation after generation, for a modernity that, like Samuel Beckett's Godot, never arrives.

I am aware my argument leaves open at least two related questions. The first: Is it that our task as intellectuals consists, then, simply in announcing and celebrating our collective self-negation in the face of the "popular" or the "subaltern"? I think that the perspective I am arguing for can and should lead to another possibility, one that would involve something like a "critique of academic reason," a critique that comes from *within* the academy and our professional and pedagogical responsibilities in it. By its very nature, this possibility would have to take the form of what used to be called, in a language that is hopefully not totally nostalgic or irrelevant, criticism/self-criticism. The goal of that self-criticism would be to encourage or deepen the possibility of an alliance between the progressive sectors of the intelligentsia and the social movements.

The second question has to do with myself in particular, as someone who writes in the U.S. academy about (*sobre*), and not from (*desde*) Latin America. What does it mean for a citizen of the United States to propose that Latin America should define itself, "in the years that lie before us," to recall Hegel's phrase, in an antagonistic relationship with his own country? My provisional answer is similar to Huntington's in his final book, *Who Are We?*, which concerns the effects of Hispanic immigration on the future of the United States as a unified nation-state: the "clash of civilizations" is now internal to the United States; or, to put this another way, the future of the United States is no longer located *within* the United States. In order to create a United States that can bring to fruition its immense democratic, egalitarian, and multicultural possibility, the articulation of Latin America as an alternative to, instead of an extension of, the United States is a historical necessity. To articulate Latin America as a "civilization," however, is not only to articulate a territoriality that is purely external or antagonistic to the United States. Latin America, "nuestra América," in José Martí's phrase, is not "outside" North America; it extends deeply *into* North or "Anglo" America. This was already the case during the era of Martí and Rodó at the end of the nineteenth century, but it is even more so today, as Huntington laments. The dialectic of the master and the slave teaches that the reality of the master is found in the slave, whose apparent capitulation is the source of his sense of privilege and authority; because of this, the master suffers from an "unhappy consciousness," as Hegel put it in the *Phenomenology*. The belligerent imperialism of the United States in the wake of 9/11, now alleviated but by no means transcended by Obama, and the continuing reaction against undocumented immigrants represent the dominion of this "unhappy consciousness" over our national spirit and destiny. The ability of the United States to pass beyond this impasse in its own national life does not lie within the United States itself; it depends on the full emancipation of Latin America *as Latin America*, including that part of Latin America that has been, from the very beginning of the nation, *within* the United States. But that emancipation, in turn, will require an inversion or redefinition of the relationship between the United States and Latin America.

That means, I think, recognizing that the United States—a *certain* United States—has entered a period of decline, and that Latin America—a *certain* Latin America—is in a still precarious period of historical ascendancy.

The Persistence of the Nation
(against *Empire*)

EMPIRE AND MULTITUDE   If Michael Hardt and Antonio Negri are right, and we are in something like a new Roman Empire, in which there is no longer a center or periphery (for the Empire has no outside), then the central question of our times might be: Who are the Christians today? That is, who in the world today, within Empire but not *of* it, like the early Christians, carries the possibility of a logic that is opposed to Empire and that will bring about its eventual downfall or transformation?[1]

Even for those who continue to consider themselves Marxists in some sense (and I include myself in that category), it no longer seems enough to call this subject the proletariat or the working class. Hardt and Negri themselves prefer the idea of the "multitude"—which they derive from Spinoza via the Italian political philosopher Paolo Virno. Hardt and Negri have themselves suggested on various occasions postcolonial studies and subaltern studies in particular as one of their inspirations.[2] This gesture has the positive effect of opening up the category of the subaltern to the future, instead of seeing it, as Gramsci did, as an identity shaped by the resistance of rural tradition to modernity. Are the categories of the subaltern and the multitude commensurate, such that one could imagine a sort of strategic convergence between the projects of Hardt and Negri in *Empire* and subaltern studies, particularly around the critique of the nation-state?[3]

Yes and no. There is a perhaps crucial difference between the multitude and the subaltern: the multitude, as Hardt and Negri use the term, is meant to designate a faceless or rather many-faced, hydra-headed, hybrid collective subject conjured up by globalization and cultural deterritori-alization, whereas the subaltern is in the first place a specific identity as such, "whether this is expressed in terms of class, caste, age, gender and office or in any other way," to recall Ranajit Guha's classic definition.[4] It follows that the politics of the subaltern must be, at least in some measure, "identity" politics.

The problem here is that Hardt and Negri themselves go to some pains in *Empire* to argue that multicultural identity politics as they understand it (that is, as what usually is called "liberal multiculturalism") is itself deeply complicit with Empire. For if supra- or subnational permeability is the central economic characteristic of the new global capitalism, then multicultural heterogeneity is syntonic with this permeability in some ways, exploding or reordering at the level of the ideological superstruc-ture previously hegemonic narratives of the unified nation-state and the "people" (*one* language, history, territoriality, etc.).

For Machiavelli, who could be said to have been the first modern thinker of national liberation struggle, "the people" (*il popolo*) is the con-dition for the nation and, in turn, realizes itself as a collective subject in the nation. What Hardt's and Negri's concept of the multitude implies is that in effect you can have "the people" without the nation. Machiavelli be-lieved that "the people" without the nation is irremediably heterogeneous and servile—like the Jews in Egyptian captivity. It is the Prince—Moses—who confers on "the people" a unity of will and identity by making it into a nation. But the appeal to the idea of the nation also stabilizes that will and identity—as, now, *a* people—around a hegemonic vision, codified in the law and the state apparatus, of a common language, set of values, cul-ture, interests, community, tasks, sacrifices, historical destiny—a vision that rhetorically sutures over the gaps and discontinuities internal to "the people." But it is in those gaps and discontinuities that the force of the subaltern or the subaltern-as-multitude appears.

Is the transcendence of the nation-state by globalization fortuitous for the project of human emancipation and diversity, then? Hardt and Negri, following a tradition of Marxist antinationalism that goes back to Rosa Luxemburg (and in some ways Marx himself), seem to think that it is. Their argument against multiculturalism in *Empire* is connected to their argument against hegemony in Gramsci's sense of "moral and intellectual leadership of the nation." They want to imagine a form of politics that would go beyond the limits of both the nation and the forms of political and cultural representation traditionally bound up with the idea of hegemony—a politics of "constituent power," as they call it. Thus, for example:

> The multitude is self-organization. Certainly, there must be a moment when reappropriation and self-organization reach a threshold and configure a real event. This is when the political is really affirmed—when the genesis is complete and self-valorization, the cooperative convergence of subjects, and the proletarian management of production become a constituent power. This is the point when the modern republic ceases to exist and the postmodernist posse arises. This is the founding moment of an earthly city that is strong and distinct from any divine city. The capacity to construct places, temporalities, migrations, and new bodies already affirms its hegemony through the actions of the multitude against the Empire. (*Empire*, 411)

But where would this "capacity to construct places, temporalities, migrations, and new bodies" come from, if not from subjectivities defined by (subaltern) "identity"? *Empire* seems to move at times into a post-political register altogether, which depends paradoxically, in the fashion of Marx's and Engels's "All that is solid melts into air," on the radicalizing power of capital itself, seen as the outcome of collective labor, to both transform and transnationalize the proletariat, in the process bursting apart the integument of the nation-state and allowing for the emergence of new forms of political activity and mobilization. One of these new forms, Hardt and Negri argue, appears around the question of the population displacements produced by globalization. Mass immigration reveals the antagonism of the multitude—the subject both engendered by and opposed to global capital—and the anachronistic system of national borders. From this it follows for them that the demand for global citizenship, founded on the general right to control one's movement, is the multitude's ultimate demand.

This is certainly a legitimate demand, as is the related demand for a universal social wage. It is hard, though, to see it as a demand—even what Trotskyists used to call a "transitional demand" (a demand for a reform that if met would produce a chain of progressively more radical demands)—that would explode the limits of global capital or its emerging political-ideological superstructure. Rather, it seems that global capital is the precondition for both making and fulfilling that demand. For Hardt and Negri, the multitude is an "expanded" way of naming the proletariat that does not limit it to the category of productive wage labor, a way of seeing the proletariat instead as a hybrid or heterogeneous subject conjured up by, but always/already in excess of, capitalism at its present stage. We know, of course, that the idea of the subaltern played a similar role for Gramsci in the *Prison Notebooks*, beyond its usefulness as a euphemism to placate the prison censors. But how much of the radical potential they attribute to the multitude is, at least in part, a resistance to coming under formal or real subsumption in capitalist relations of production, that is, to becoming proletarianized? Isn't the distance or incommensurability between the "proletariat" as a category (defined by formal or real subsumption in capitalist relations of production) and the multitude—that is, between abstract and real labor—a difference marked precisely by, or as, "identity"? If this is so, then the question of multiculturalism and "identity" moves from the status of a secondary contradiction to become the, or a, main contradiction.

Hardt and Negri seem to approximate a recognition of the crucial role of identity, or, as they put it, "singularity," when they write: "The multitude affirms its singularity by inverting the ideological illusion that all humans on the global surfaces of the world market are interchangeable. Standing the ideology of the market on its feet, the multitude promotes through its labor the biopolitical singularizations of groups and sets of humanity, across each and every node of global exchange" (*Empire*, 395). But there is an ambiguity here. Is it that Hardt and Negri are noting the emergence of new logics of the social that oppose or resist the homogenizing effects of market capitalism in the name of (previously constituted?) "singularities," which now acquire in the face of capital a force of radical negativity? Or is the generalization and abstraction of labor power produced by the commodification of human labor the precondition for "biopolitical singularizations of groups"? In the second case, their argument, though it appears in a postmodernist guise, is essentially similar to that of orthodox Marxism (to be specific, it resembles in some ways Karl Kautsky's idea of superimperialism). To be against capitalism, one must first have to be transformed by it. There can be no resistance to *becoming* proletarianized, only resistance from the position of being always/already subject to capital. Hardt and Negri write: "The telos of the multitude must live and organize its political space against Empire and within the 'maturity of the times' and the ontological conditions that Empire presents" (407). But this is to subordinate the struggle against capital to the temporal unfolding of capital itself. What the equation of the multitude and early Christianity suggests, instead, is that new/old forms of temporality, which are not the time of capital, or Empire, need to express themselves. The telos of the multitude is, in the last instance, opposed to the telos of Empire, even as it arises within it (the same problematic marks the relation of capitalism and socialism). If what the multitude resists is the "interchangeability" that results from the general commodification of labor and nature, then what it affirms as singularity are forms of cultural and psychic difference, time, need, and desire that are at odds with the "ontological conditions that Empire presents."

Hardt and Negri borrow Paolo Virno's metaphor of "Exodus" to describe the detachment of the multitude from the nation-state, envisioning a movement from the "modern republic" to the "postmodernist posse." But an Exodus to where ? (Because Exodus is also for Virno "the foundation of a Republic.")[5] If the demand for global citizenship has a slightly reformist air, there is a more militant antagonism to Empire that is revealed for Hardt and Negri in spontaneous and punctual acts of insurgency like the Los Angeles riots, the Zapatista rebellion in Chiapas, Seattle, or the Intifada. Christians versus Rome, in other words. Yet all of these movements are deeply embedded in one form or other of identity politics. Early Christianity was an ideology—indeed, it served Althusser as the very model of ideology. As such it had to create new kinds of territoriality within the Empire (I understand territoriality to designate the relation between personal identity and space). What were the territorialities it created? Initially the scattered "communities" of believers represented in the Epistles (Romans, Corinthians, Philippians, Ephesians . . .), but eventually, out of those communities, and with the breakdown of the Empire (a breakdown in part due to their proliferation), nations, or at least the basis for the modern European nation-states.

If we put the question of multiculturalism and the question of the limits of the nation together, it becomes apparent that without the capacity to interpellate hegemonically the nation (which could be either an actual or possible nation), identity politics has no other option than to be part of "the cultural logic of late capitalism" (to recall Fredric Jameson's phrase), because it simply expresses what is already the case, indeed even desirable, within the rules of the game of the world market system and liberal democracy, rather than something that is driven to contravene those rules. Its radical potential as a site for mobilization against the power and hegemony of global capital therefore depends on the nation. Outside that territoriality it becomes what Coco Fusco calls "happy multiculturalism"—that is, an aspect of the ideological superstructure of globalized capital itself.

But the same criticism could be made of the idea of the multitude. If it cannot address itself to an instance of hegemony, is the action of the multitude political at all, or simply a kind of turbulence created and tolerated by the generalization of market relations (in such a way that neoliberalism might seem a better ideological expression of the multitude's reality than communism or socialism), and in any case controllable by military and police operations? An earlier Marxism in Latin America supposed that what was called the "Indian question" would be solved through the proletarianization and acculturation of the indigenous peoples of the continent. José Carlos Mariátegui was one of the first to argue against this conception, noting that the bases for socialism could also be found in both pre-Columbian and contemporary features of precapitalist indigenous Andean societies. A testimonial text like *I, Rigoberta Menchú*, similarly, forces the reader to recognize that the participation of indigenous groups in the armed struggle in Guatemala was directed in part against, or to limit, their proletarianization and acculturation/transculturation into modernity. As Menchú herself has explained on numerous occasions, this is not exactly the same thing as a rejection of modernity or science/technology as it is sometimes made out to be by critics of multiculturalism and postmodernist relativism—the testimonial text is itself a form of secularized literary modernity. Rather, it is an insistence that modernity come *on their terms*. Ideologically, therefore, that insistence required both in the period of armed struggle and after it an affirmation of indigenous "identity": values, languages, customs, dress, and territoriality (especially crucial in this regard in *I, Rigoberta Menchú* is the defense of communal land rights).

Hardt and Negri include indigenous struggles such as those represented in *I, Rigoberta Menchú* in their concept of the multitude. But then the question remains: Are what they understand by ideological dynamics of the multitude the same thing as the ideological dynamics that actually motivate these struggles? Or have they subsumed those dynamics in their concept of the multitude, which risks becoming, like the orthodox Marxist concept of the proletariat, another "universal" subject?

THE NATION AND MODERNITY There has been some effort to revive Leninism lately—most notably perhaps by Slavoj Žižek. But the aspect of Lenin's thought that deserves continued attention in relation to our concerns here is not one that someone like Žižek, who shares Hardt's and Negri's rejection of multiculturalism and identity politics, would approve of. That is so because it has to do with what was called in classical Marxism the "national question," which is, of course, at heart a question of national "identity." But what is a national identity: an identity as one and the same, or an identity as many and diverse?

To recall briefly Lenin's argument: In the stage of monopoly capitalism, based on competition for raw materials and labor supply between national capitalisms, the main contradiction shifts from the capital-labor contradiction within the territoriality of given nation-states to the conflict between dominated and dominant capitalist nations or national groups. The main form of anticapitalist struggle in turn shifts from class-based unions and parties—the organizations of the second International—to national liberation struggles, preferably led by the working class, but not limited to working-class interests as such.

It could be argued that underlying the conflict between the so-called free world and communism in the Cold War was a deeper conflict between forces of globalizing capitalism, based in but no longer strictly limited to the nation-state, and those of ethnic nationalism. If that is true, then the political and strategic contradiction between capitalism and communism consisted in the fact that communism acted essentially as a proxy and support for nationalism. A case could be made similarly that the problem of the nation and of national identity is still at the heart of global conflict, even though the nature of that conflict has shifted in the last quarter century. It is thus perhaps best to respond to the claim underlying *Empire* that the nation form has been, or is in the process of being, transcended by the present stage of capitalism, which no longer requires that form in the way monopoly capital did (such that competition between respective national capitals was also military competition between nation-states): it is too early to tell. It may be that the partial disabling of the economic autonomy of the nation-state by globalization and the sometimes disastrous consequences this produces may in some ways lend a new intensity and urgency to the national or the local.

Lenin's argument about the "national question" represents his most original and politically charged contribution to Marxist theory, in the sense that it introduces the possibility of cultural determination into classical Marxism, at the same time locating that cultural determination within the parameters of a historical materialism—that is, in the particularity of the imperialist form of capitalism (significantly, it is the aspect of Lenin's thought that Žižek all but completely passes over, preferring to dwell instead on the, for me, less original and less fortunate concepts of the vanguard party and the "dictatorship of the proletariat"). But, in the way it specifically articulates the idea of national liberation struggle, Lenin's argument is not particularly useful for taking up the question of the nation today—that is, as a question not only about what nations have been but about what they might become—in what Lenin himself would probably have agreed is a new stage of capitalism.

The Russian empire was, in Lenin's image, the "prison-house of nations." In thinking about what constituted a nation, however, Lenin (and thence Stalin in his famous 1914 essay on the National Question) took over the conventional social-democratic idea—articulated by his mentor and rival Kautsky—that a nation was a permanent and relatively homogeneous community of language, territory, market, economy, psychology, and culture. Soviet nationalities policy followed more or less this conception, aiming at a "union" of nominally independent republics, each built around a single dominant national or ethnic group, despite evident problems (what to do about Soviet Jews, for example, who were a people without a specific territoriality) and adjustments dictated by Stalinist realpolitik (deportation or relocation of ethnic groups deemed hostile to the Soviet project; settlement of Russian minorities in other "nations"; etc.). The notion of the nation itself as "multinational"—that is, multicultural—was rejected by Lenin and the Bolsheviks as "reformist." One can see in this conception the seeds of the breakup of both the Soviet Union and Yugoslavia, which both showed a tendency to fracture precisely along the "national" lines affirmed in the constitution of the various republics.

The alternative position in early twentieth-century Marxism was articulated in 1907 by the Austro-Marxist Otto Bauer in his treatise *The*

Question of Nationalities and Social Democracy (Lenin commissioned Stalin to write his essay on the national question in response to Bauer). Reflecting the multilinguistic and multiethnic character of the Austro-Hungarian Empire then in decay (Bauer's plural "nationalities" is itself significant in contrast to the Bolshevik insistence on "the national question"), Bauer was concerned with the problem of minorities that, like the Russian Jews, possessed attributes of nationhood—what Bauer called a "community of will"—but not an independent territorial state founded on those attributes. He set up the following problematic in this regard:

1. National or ethnic identities—"communities of will"—are not simply ideological hallucinations or forms of false-consciousness, as the antinationalist position in Marxism and anarchism argued, but are themselves the determinate products of the impact of capitalist combined and uneven development on different populations. They amount to what in sociological terms could be characterized as a contradiction between (national-ethnic) Gemeinschaft versus (capitalist-modern) Gesellschaft.

2. In a liberal-democratic state national or ethnic multiculturalism may be tolerated in principle but in practice is always limited by the hegemony of a dominant nation or ethnic group.

3. Therefore, the same principle of self-determination that legitimizes the existing nation-state and the hegemony of the dominant national or ethnic group may then be used by disaffected minorities to demand states where they would be a majority.

4. But should these disaffected minorities become states?

Bauer's response to this problematic was to divorce the "community of will" of language, group experience, and psychology or "national character" from territoriality defined explicitly as "national" in the conventional sense reflected in the Kautsky-Lenin position (i.e., exhibiting a community of language, market, etc.), by imagining democratically organized forms of relative national autonomy and self-determination for national or ethnic minorities, within a larger territoriality, which, however, would also be a nation, or, to use Bauer's own term, a "multinational state" in some sense or other. As the editor of the recent reedition of *The Question of Nationalities* in English remarks, Bauer challenges in effect the main assumptions of the contemporary world of nation-states: to wit, "that sovereignty is unitary and indivisible, that national self-determination requires the constitution of separate nation-states, and that nation-states are the only recognized international players."[6]

There is much that seems dated in Bauer's argument today; but there is also a basic impulse that seems worth reconsidering. In a world marked by mass immigration and/or articulation of national or group identities over previous forms of territoriality, national or otherwise, Bauer's proposal has the advantage of redefining radically the problem of minority populations within or between existing nation-states, since no population group is "national" as such, nor does nationalism mean necessarily national "exclusivity." One might see Bauer in this regard as the first theoretician of multiculturalism rather than cultural-linguistic-legal homogeneity as the basis for the identity of the nation. This makes him also one of the first Marxists after Marx to think outside the framework of a normative modernity.

That is an important achievement, because in many ways the argument between capitalism and socialism that framed the Cold War was essentially an argument about which of the two systems could best carry forward the possibility of a political, scientific, cultural, and economic modernity latent in capitalism itself. The basic premise of Marxism as a modernizing ideology was that bourgeois society could not complete its own promise of emancipation and material well-being, given the contradictions inherent in the capitalist mode of production, contradictions above all between the social character of the forces of production and the private character of ownership and capital accumulation. Freeing the forces of production from the fetters of capitalist relations of production—so the familiar argument went—the state socialist or quasi-socialist regimes inspired by the Soviet model would soon overcome these limitations, inaugurating an era of unprecedented economic growth, which in turn would be the material precondition for socialism and eventually the transition to communism. The—at least for the moment triumphant—response of capitalism was that the force of the free market would be more dynamic and efficient in the long run in producing modernity and economic growth.

What was not in question on either side of this argument, however, was the desirability of modernity as such. In turn, the various forms of nationalism shared this consensus (that is why dependency theory became the underlying political economy of nationalism). Habermas's concept of communicative rationality expresses the prospect of a society that is, or that could become, transparent to itself. As Bauer realized almost a century earlier, however, what opposes transparency or the universalization of communicative rationality is not only the conflict of tradition and modernity—that is, the "incompleteness" of modernity, to borrow Habermas's own phrase—but also the intensification of forms of social heterogeneity and difference produced in part by the very process of capitalist modernity itself. Bauer's problem was to imagine the project of the Left as detached from the telos of modernity, particularly as it is incarnated in the "history" of the nation-state.

What is at stake in this question is the relationship between subalternity, narrative history, and the time of capital. Dipesh Chakrabarty formulates the problem in the following way:

> Subaltern histories written with an eye to difference cannot constitute yet another attempt, in the long and universalistic tradition of "socialist" histories, to help erect the subaltern as the subject of modern democracies, that is, to expand the history of the modern in such a way as to make it more representative of society as a whole. . . . Stories about how this or that group in Asia, Africa, or Latin America resisted the "penetration" of capitalism do not, in this sense, constitute "subaltern" history, for these narratives are predicated on imagining a space that is external to capital—the chronologically "before" of capital—but that is at the same time a part of a historicist, unitary time frame within which both the "before" and "after" of capitalist production can unfold. The "outside" I am thinking of is different from what is simply imagined as "before or after capital" in historicist prose. This "outside" I think of, following Derrida, as something attached to the category "capital" itself, something that straddles a border zone of temporality, that conforms to the temporal code within which "capital" comes into being even as it violates that code, something we are able to see only because we can think/theorize capital, but that also always reminds us that other temporalities, other forms of worlding, coexist and are possible. . . . Subaltern studies, as I think of it, can only situate itself theoretically at the juncture where we give up neither Marx nor "difference," for, as I have said, the resistance it speaks of is something that can happen only *within* the time horizon of capital and yet has to be thought of as something that disrupts the unity of that time. Unconcealing the tension between real and abstract labor ensures that capital/commodity has heterogeneities and incommensurabilities inscribed in its core.[7]

The equation between the nation-state and the modern rests on the fact that the problem of the state is to incorporate its population into its own modernity. The population — or sectors of the population — "lags behind" modernity (expressed as instrumental or bureaucratic reason). What the concept of ungovernability expresses is the incommensurability between what Chakrabarty calls the "radical heterogeneity" of the subaltern and the reason of state. Ungovernability is the space of recalcitrance, disobedience, marginality, anachronism, insurgency. But ungovernability also designates the failure of formal politics and of the nation — that is, of hegemony. In this sense, like Hardt's and Negri's multitude, the subaltern has a differential relation with the nation: it is "below" or "in excess" of the nation. It "interrupts" the "modern" narrative of the transition from feudalism to capitalism, the formation and consolidation of the nation-state, and the teleological passage through the different "stages" of capitalism (merchant, competitive, monopoly, imperialist, now global).

The privileging in postmodernist social theory of the concept of civil society might be seen as connected to this argument from subaltern studies, since it is founded on a disillusion with the capacity of the state to organize society and to produce modernity in either a capitalist or socialist form. But it would be a mistake to assume that the subaltern is necessarily coextensive with civil society. That is because the idea of civil society in its usual sense (Hegel's *burgerlich Gesellschaft*) is also tied, like the nation-state, to a narrative of "development" or "unfolding" (*Entwicklung*, to use the word favored by both Kant and Hegel), which by virtue of its own requirements (formal education, literacy and scientific and technical education, nuclear family units, party politics, business, private property) excludes significant sectors of the population from full citizenship or limits their access to citizenship. That exclusion or limitation is what constitutes the subaltern.

It follows that what Chakrabarty calls the "politics of despair" of the subaltern may be driven by a resistance to or skepticism not only about the official nation-state but also about what constitutes civil society. The equation of civil society, culture, and hegemony in Gramsci and other thinkers of modernity runs up against the problem that subaltern negativity is often directed precisely against what is understood and valued as "culture" by dominant groups. This line of thought might seem at first sight to be a variation of Gramsci's point about the possible noncoincidence between "the people" and the nation (that noncoincidence, to repeat, is what the concept of the subaltern designates). But the crisis of the nation-state is also the crisis of the solution Gramsci sought to this problem: that is, the idea of the national-popular hegemony. Hegemony itself is seen by cultural studies theorists like Homi Bhabha or Néstor García Canclini as founded on an outmoded distinction that links subalternity to premodern and hegemony to modern forms of culture. In contemporary societies, so García Canclini's argument in particular goes, the tradition/modernity binary dissolves, and thus along with it the dichotomy subalternity/hegemony.[8]

Hardt and Negri borrow from cultural studies the idea that the category that expresses the dynamic of popular culture is hybridity more than subalternity. Hardt has written about the "end of civil society," tied as it is to the form of the nation. Cultural studies suggests a new, transnational form of civil society, based on diaspora, deterritorialization, and hybridization. If hybridization is coextensive with civil society in its national form, however, the binary that is not deconstructed by cultural studies is the one that is constitutive of this normative (as opposed to descriptive) value of hybridity: that is, the state/civil society dichotomy itself, where civil society is seen as the place where hybridity appears, as against the monological and homogenizing discourse of the nation-state. Thus, in seeking "democratically" to displace hermeneutic authority from bourgeois high culture to popular reception and "crossovers," cultural studies ends up in some ways legitimizing the market and globalization. The very cultural logic it represents points in the direction of assuming that hegemony is no longer a possibility, because there no longer exists a common cultural basis for forming the collective national-popular subject required to exercise hegemony. There are only deterritorialized identities or identities in the process of becoming deterritorialized.

The generalization of the time of capital that globalization entails tends toward a single, overarching temporality—that of the circulation of commodities and "the end of history"—in which other historicities continue to exist simply as elements of pastiche. Fredric Jameson explains magic realism as entailing the coexistence in a given social formation of temporalities and value systems corresponding to different modes of production that bleed through each other, in the manner of a palimpsest.[9] If there was implicit in the idea of the melting pot or, in Latin American nationalism, *mestizaje*, a teleological narrative of the adaptation of "the people" to the state (and vice versa), a similar (albeit often unacknowledged), but now postnational teleology operates in the concept of hybridity/hybridization in cultural studies, since it designates a dialectical process—seen as both inevitable and providential—of the "overcoming" of antinomies that are rooted in the immediate cultural and historical past, including the "past" of high modernism itself. Despite its gestures to postmodernism, then, cultural studies simply transfers the dynamic of modernization from the sphere of modernist high culture and the state ideological apparatuses to mass culture, now seen as more capable of producing "cultural citizenship." In this sense, cultural studies does not break with the values of modernity and does not, in itself, point beyond the limits of neoliberal hegemony. The positivist epistemology and politics (alternatively social democratic or neo-Leninist) of the "left" critics of multiculturalism and nationalism, and the discourse of civil society and hybridity mobilized by cultural studies in response to the "flows" of economic and cultural globalization are two sides of the same coin: forms of the rationality of a capitalist modernity in which "traditional" identities and value systems now seen as anachronistic, including "national" identities as such, should disappear or be sublated in a new "mix."

IDENTITY POLITICS AND RADICAL MULTICULTURALISM   We return, then, to what Chakrabarty calls the "radical heterogeneity" of the subaltern. Is the exteriority of the subaltern as an "identity" simply a function of its anachronism, or does it represent a contradictory alterity within modernity—"something that conforms to the temporal code within which capital comes into being while violating that code at the same time," to recall the passage from Chakrabarty that I cited earlier (that is, different logics of the social and different modes of experiencing and conceptualizing history and value within the time of capital and the territoriality of the nation-state)? Identity politics in general is in bad odor in the higher reaches of academic theory (though not so much in politics on the ground), a consensus opinion that Hardt and Negri eagerly participate in. (Perhaps the strongest form of this rejection is Žižek's well-known claim that multiculturalism is the "ideal form" of global capitalism.) No one doubts that multicultural demands for "recognition" can lead to new, apartheid-like forms of territoriality tolerated and in some cases even encouraged by both local states and the international system: it was after all precisely the intention of the apartheid regime in South Africa in creating legally autonomous and "self-determined" tribal states—the Bantustans—to avoid by this means the prospect that the majority black and colored population of the country could form a political majority.

The philosophical case against identity politics was made forcefully by Wendy Brown in her book *State of Injury* (1995). Let me quote her argument at some length, because I think it is representative of the consensus against identity politics in critical theory I allude to above:

> In its emergence as a protest against marginalization or subordination, politicized identity . . . becomes attached to its own exclusion both because it is premised on this exclusion for its existence as identity and because the identity as the site of exclusion, as exclusion, augments or "alters the direction of the suffering" entailed in subordination or marginalization by finding a site of blame for it. But in so doing, it installs pain over its unredeemed history in the very foundation of its political claim, in its demand for recognition as identity. In locating a site of blame for its powerlessness over its past—a past of injury, a past as a hurt will—and locating a "reason" for the "unendurable pain" of social powerlessness in the present, it converts this reasoning into an ethnicizing politics, a politics of recrimination that seeks to avenge the hurt even while it reaffirms it, discursively codifies it. Politicized identity thus enunciates itself, makes claims for itself, only by entrenching, restating, dramatizing, and inscribing its pain in politics; it can hold out no future—for itself or others—that triumphs over this pain. The loss of historical direction, and with it the loss of futurity characteristic of the late modern age, is thus homologically refigured in the structure of desire of the dominant political expression of the age: identity politics.[10]

There is more than a trace here (as in Hardt and Negri too) of Nietzsche's critique of Christianity as "slave morality." Brown presupposes that identity politics cannot aspire to be hegemonic without losing its raison d'être, that subaltern negativity can only affirm impotence, resentment, suffering, and revenge: a simple inversion of the existing order ("the first shall be last and the last first"). One thing, however, is identity politics without the transformative possibility of hegemonic articulation—that is, within the rules of the game of the dominant bourgeois-liberal political-legal-cultural institutions and practices;[11] another is identity politics as the articulating principle of a new kind of "alliance politics" that can contend for hegemony within the territoriality of the nation-state. That is so in part because even the prospect of attaining hegemony would necessarily transform the subaltern identities that enter into play in a process of

CHAPTER TWO

hegemonic articulation. But if the subaltern has to become like that which is already hegemonic in order to become itself hegemonic, then what will have been gained? Obviously, it must affirm *something* of that "injured" identity (as subaltern, marginal, excluded, discriminated against, "hurt") that launched it into struggle in the first place. It cannot enter into politics simply by renouncing or "deconstructing" its identity claims without also affirming a fictive universalist "humanism" that is itself part and parcel of the ideology of the existing forms of hegemony.

What is potentially radical and transformative in multicultural identity politics, what makes it a crucial arena for the formation of "constituent power," then, is not so much the desire for "recognition" or to have "a room of one's own," but rather the way these demands propose to redefine the identity of both the nation and the international order: that is, they are radical to the extent that they seek to *universalize* their singularity. To do so, they must pass through the state.

In Frantz Fanon's succinct definition, the nation-state is a "bourgeois contrivance," and we would do well not to overlook this. But it would also be a kind of essentialism to argue that the idea of the nation-state as such is limited to only one form of class rule, and it would be short-sighted to found a political alternative to globalization on the negation of contradictions within nations or between nations that are in one way or another contradictions about national identity and values. That negation would amount to a postmodernist inversion of the now properly discredited argument that in national liberation struggles women, gays, workers, peasants, and others have to suspend their specific demands in favor of national "unity" against a common enemy. What might be envisioned in the place of both classical nineteenth-century style nationalism and more recent populist forms of nationalism is a new kind of politics that interpellates "the people" not as a unitary, homogeneously modern subject, but rather, in the fashion of Bauer's "communities of will," as internally fissured, heterogeneous, multiple. To put this another way, the unity and mutual reciprocity of the elements of the subject Hardt and Negri designate as the multitude depend on a recognition of sociocultural difference and incommensurability—an affirmation, that is, of "contradictions among the people," within in the first place an existing (or possible) nation, which does preclude seeing that nation and segments of its population as involved in a larger confederation of nations (as in, to mention only two cases, dual citizenship, or indigenous territoriality that crosses existing national borders). Socialism would be the social and economic form of this difference and incommensurability, promoting from them the concrete institutions and practices of an egalitarian society, but without resolving them into a transcendent or unitary cultural or political logic.

In the concluding volume of the "Empire" trilogy, *Commonwealth*, Hardt and Negri take account of Bolivian social movements such as the *cocaleros*, indigenous rights groups, or the coalition against the privatization of municipal water in Cochabamba as concrete examples of what they mean by the multitude. They note correctly that these movements "paved the way for the election of Evo Morales to the presidency in 2005" (108–12). But they decline to discuss what has happened in Bolivia since then: that is, what happens when social movements originating well outside the state lend themselves to a process of hegemonic articulation that culminates in their occupation of the state. That is because Hardt and Negri share with neoliberalism a critique of the nation-state, which they see as an obstacle to the insurgency of the multitude in the new, postnational global order. My point here, by contrast, is that to construct the politics of the multitude today, under conditions of globalization and in the face of the neoliberal critique and privatization of state functions, requires a relegitimization and reterritorialization of the nation-state. But, of course, such a relegitimization would also require, at the same time, new concepts of the nation, of "national" identity and interests, of citizenship and democracy, of the "national-popular," and thus finally of politics itself. That possibility, which it seems to me is fundamental for both the emergence and survival of the political project represented by the Latin American marea rosada (and beyond it), underlies all of the essays that make up this book. But I will return to it most explicitly in the last of them, "The Subaltern and the State."

Deconstruction and Latinamericanism (apropos Alberto Moreiras's *The Exhaustion of Difference*)

Alberto Moreiras's *The Exhaustion of Difference* was one of the most wide-ranging and influential books in the field of Latin American literary and cultural studies in the period immediately preceding and following 9/11.[1] I would like to use it here to reflect more generally on the relation between deconstruction and Latinamericanism. I should begin by saying that this relation is a complex one, in the sense that deconstruction functions in this relation as both a *critique* but also a new *form* of Latinamericanism.[2]

The Exhaustion of Difference follows or anticipates a cluster of publications that shared this double ambition, some by former students or associates of Moreiras—for example, Idelber Avelar's *The Untimely Present*, Gareth Williams's *The Other Side of the Popular*, Brett Levinson's *The Ends of Literature*, or Patrick Dove's *The Catastrophe of Modernity*—and others by the group of writers and critics associated with Nelly Richard's *Revista de Crítica Cultural* in Chile, among them Diamela Eltit, Willy Thayer, Federico Galende, Sergio Villalobos, Kemy Oyarzún, and Richard herself. Though it would be too much to speak here of a "school," one could speak perhaps of a collective "intervention" along certain lines of theoretical and personal affinity, which I perhaps too restrictively characterize here as deconstruction. Kate Jenckes has dubbed this intervention the "New Latin Americanism," alluding to the project of the New Americanism in American studies, which was also indebted to deconstruction in some ways.[3] She intends the phrase to describe the work of Moreiras and the North American–based group in particular (which she is herself part of), but it could be extended to include the Chilean group as well: the boundaries between the two groups have been relatively porous.

The approximation of deconstruction and Latinamericanism has its roots in an earlier, "first-wave" critical articulation, of which perhaps the most celebrated example was Sylvia Molloy's book *Signs of Borges*. It also includes more generally the work of what might be called the "Yale school" in Latin American literary criticism (which of course is not limited to nor coextensive with critics actually at or from Yale); for example (to cite just a few particularly influential texts), Roberto González Echevarría's *Voice of the Masters* and *Myth and Archive*, Djelal Kadir's *Questing Fictions*, Carlos Alonso's *The Latin American Regional Novel*, and Doris Sommer's *Foundational Fictions*. As I noted in the introduction, Moreiras himself argues that the foundational gesture of Latinamericanist deconstruction was Enrico Mario Santí's notion of the relation between Latinamericanist discourse, which Santí conceived of on the model of Said's idea of Orientalism, and what he called, taking the term from Geoffrey Hartmann, "restitutional excess."

Politically, the character of this first-wave intervention of deconstruction in the Latin American field was ambiguous. On the whole its practitioners could be described as sympathizers of the Left or left-liberals, although in some cases they took a position that was more explicitly critical of the Left (Santí and González Echevarría, for example, were products of Cuban exile culture after the revolution). What is undoubtedly the case, however, was that more often than not what was deconstructed in the work of first-wave deconstruction were the claims of certain forms of literary and literary-critical discourse associated with the nationalist or populist left in Latin America, or with positions of "solidarity" with Latin America from abroad, to "speak for" the Latin American subject.[4]

There is a continuity (most notably, around the critique of supposedly naive readings of *testimonio*) between this first wave, which breaks in the late 1980s and early 1990s, and the "second-wave" variant of deconstruction represented by *The Exhaustion of Difference* and the New Latin Americanism in the late 1990s and first decade of the new century. What is "new" about the New Latin Americanism, however, and what it has in common with Gayatri Spivak and with Derrida himself (though not with de Man or Yale school criticism generally), is that it sees its intervention as a force for the renewal of, if not the Left in a traditional sense, then certainly an emancipatory politics to come in the emerging new world order of globalization. Moreiras calls this "a thinking for the interregnum" (90–91), borrowing an idea from Paul Bové, who understands by "the interregnum" the period between the disappearance of the bipolar order of the Cold War and modernity and the consolidation of the new transnational order of global capitalism. More specifically, Moreiras claims: "My intention is not merely critical; it is also preparatory. If there is to be a politics of Latin American cultural studies that may have a chance of grasping what the political is, in other words, a politics that would not be merely administration, but one that could conceivably have some effect in preparing a transformation, I believe it must be articulated through as relentless and savage a practice of clearing as possible" (299).

That claim—to have "some effect in preparing a transformation"—would seem to make the New Latin Americanism both a theoretical-critical precursor to and a fellow traveler of the marea rosada. Why that has *not* been the case, why, on the contrary, the rise of the marea rosada has led to an impasse in the relation of deconstruction and Latinamericanism is what I want to try to understand here.

Moreiras proposes in *The Exhaustion of Difference* to use the tools of deconstruction to bring into crisis and radicalize the ideological and conceptual space of Latin American cultural studies. In that sense, the book is not a study of Latin American cultural studies as such—a concept that Moreiras uses more or less interchangeably with Latinamericanism—and even less so of Latin American popular or mass culture (in the mode of, say, Néstor García Canclini's *Culturas híbridas* or George Yúdice's *The Expediency of Culture*). It concerns rather the "politics of knowledge" involved in the representation of Latin American culture. Moreiras calls that representation "Latin Americanist thinking," understanding by that term "the sum total of academic discourse on Latin America, whether carried out in Latin America, in the United States, in Europe, or elsewhere" (*Exhaustion*, 1). Between Latinamericanism as a project of knowledge and Latin America as the object of that project, there is a "constitutive gap that is irreducible." Moreiras's argument seeks to locate itself in that gap.

Moreiras calls the sort of thinking he believes his book represents— that is, a Latinamericanist discourse that is about Latinamericanism as such—"second-order Latin Americanism." Why is this deconstructive gesture necessary in the first place? Because, Moreiras feels, "first-order" Latinamericanism, particularly in its foundational appeal to cultural nationalism and corresponding poetics/aesthetics (of magical realism, "national allegory," transculturation, hybridity, testimonial voice, etc.), is built on "outmoded" concepts of identity and difference (the adjective is his). Moreiras situates his project in the double conjuncture formed by the crisis of Latin American revolutionary nationalism and the theoretical paradigms associated with it, such as dependency theory, and the effects of globalization and neoliberal hegemony in the region, which included, of course, a relative weakening of the sovereignty of the nation-state itself (and thus apparently of the oppositional force of nationalism). For Latinamericanism to recuperate its radical political potential in the context of globalization, it needs to be pushed beyond those paradigms and its own self-satisfaction and complacency. "I have attempted throughout this book," Moreiras writes characteristically, "to move towards the aporetic moments of Latin Americanist knowledge and push Latin Americanist fulfillment against its limit" (299). For this purpose, Moreiras proposes in particular a convergence between subaltern studies and deconstruction, which depends (like Spivak in this respect) on seeing the subaltern as something that is radically exterior to both an exhausted nationalism and globalization—an "exteriority without positivity, a transhistorical remainder whose force is to appeal to an 'otherwise' understood as the negation of what hegemony negates" (298).

The deconstructivist intervention in Latinamericanism is predicated on the defeat or failure of a previous project of the Left, which it now bids to reenergize or supplant (I will come back to this point at the end of this chapter). This situation—which might be restated as how to turn mourning (mourning not only for the defeat of the Left, but also for the loss of the certainty that the discourse of that Left once represented) into resistance—had already been taken up by Moreiras in an earlier book, *Tercer espacio*.[5] *Tercer espacio* featured a series of rereadings of some of the canonical figures of Latin American modernist and postmodernist narrative (Borges, Cortázar, Lezama Lima, Elizondo, and Sarduy) in terms of this double conjuncture and in the immediate context of what came to be called "post-dictatorship." The gesture involved something more than simply repositioning the canon of modern Latin American literature in relation to the new historical and political situation of Latin America in the 1980s and 1990s; there was also in Moreiras's approach an intention to value the aesthetic and epistemological strategies developed by these writers as a form of what he called "critical regionalism" (borrowing the term from Kenneth Frampton via Fredric Jameson), capable of creating ✓ a "third space" outside of both traditional historicist/aestheticist affirmations of national-popular identity, on the one hand, and the logic of neoliberal hegemony and globalization, on the other. *Tercer espacio*, in other words, was concerned with locating the point at which aesthetic or narrative "difference" becomes both a form of resistance and a concrete possibility of an "other" or alternative modernity.

This approach (which is characteristic of the New Latin Americanism in general) affords a *strategic* importance to Latin American culture and to certain writers or texts of modern Latin American literature in particular. Indeed, literature itself—a certain sense of literature, which, in contrast to the neo-Arielist position, precisely divorces itself from its connection to the nation-state and cultural nationalism—becomes for Moreiras and the New Latin Americanists a model of how to imagine and enact a "post-hegemonic" sense of politics and community. Moreiras repeats this gesture in *The Exhaustion of Difference*. Moreiras's choice of cultural studies as his central concern was nourished by his own involvement in two major debates that dominated Latin American studies in the period immediately following the end of the Cold War. The first had to do with a shift in the power relation between the humanities and social sciences within area studies generally. The rise of cultural studies meant not only a recognition of the crisis of literary studies (traditionally a supplementary or secondary field in the policy-driven precincts of area studies), but also, paradoxically, the intrusion of literary studies and particularly "theory" (since it was mainly in literary studies that the impact of "theory" occurred) into the social sciences themselves. In response, there was a move on the part of the social sciences—particularly in history and anthropology, the disciplines most ambiguously situated between the humanities and the social sciences proper—against "taking the linguistic turn" and in favor of a neopositivistic reterritorialization of disciplinary boundaries.[6] The second debate occurred within Latin American literary and cultural theory, and concerned its "politics of location," pitting what Moreiras calls "non–Latin American Latin Americanists" writing mainly in English from the U.S. and European academy against "Latin American Latin Americanists" writing mainly in Spanish or Portuguese "from" Latin America, who saw the hegemony of the new forms of critical theory as in effect a form of intellectual colonialism or orientalization and rejected their claim to represent adequately the cultural and historical specificity of Latin America. (I will take up the question of the "politics of location" of Latinamericanism in greater detail in chapter 4.) Both of those debates, in turn, take place against the backdrop of the general crisis and transformation of universities and academic disciplines in both the United States and Latin America as a consequence of globalization and neoliberal reforms.

Moreiras properly registers the fact that the very concept of Latinamericanism is itself aporetic or undecidable. Does Latinamericanism refer to representation of knowledge about Latin America from metropolitan (mainly Spanish, Western European, or North American) universities, think tanks, and organizations like the Latin American Studies Association or does it emerge from a tradition of cultural or culturalist thought about Latin American identity and values produced in Latin America itself (what Moreiras calls "Latin American Latin Americanism"), illustrated by figures like José Carlos Mariátegui, Jorge Luis Borges, Fernando Ortiz, Rosario Castellanos, Antonio Cándido, Octavio Paz, Ángel Rama, Roberto Fernández Retamar, Antonio Cornejo Polar, Beatriz Sarlo, or Nelly Richard, who may see themselves in tension with the authority of metropolitan centers and theory. Or does it refer to knowledges and cultural practices in Latin America that are in tension with *both* non–Latin American Latinamericanism and Latin American Latinamericanism? In this third case, of course, not only Latin American literature and culture, but the name "Latin America" itself becomes problematic as a signifier of the identity of the project: for example, for indigenous peoples who constitute perhaps 20 percent of the population of what is called Latin America, and who are strictly speaking neither "American" nor "Latin," or for peasants and workers or the urban poor who may not see their own aspirations and values represented in the forms of a middle- and upper-class academic and/or literary culture that seeks to articulate a sense of "Latin American" identity—indeed, who may feel that that culture exists precisely to misrepresent and subalternize them (that is, to subalternize them precisely in the act of representing them).

The Exhaustion of Difference appears alongside two other books that also show a concern with advancing via literature the agenda of a "critical regionalism" in globalization, but in this case from South Asian subaltern studies: Dipesh Chakrabarty's *Provincializing Europe* and Gayatri Spivak's *The Death of a Discipline*. Both show several striking points of coincidence with what I have called in chapter 1 neo-Arielism. Readers of

Provincializing Europe will have been struck by a certain incommensurability between its first and second parts: the first deals with the relation between the Marxist history of capital and the—mainly religious—forms of historicity of premodern subjects, what Chakrabarty calls "the times of the gods"; the second with secular-modern Indian cultural practices of what he calls "literate upper-caste Hindu Bengalis" (19). In an extended and brilliant chapter, he describes a Bengali literary institution akin to the Spanish–Latin American literary *tertulia* called the *adda*. Chakrabarty makes the case that the adda—in its peculiar articulation of language, community, time, value, and affect—is in excess of the logic of both national and international forms of capitalism and represents therefore something like a site of a resistant or alternative modernity within global modernity. "That there should be a tension between the ideals of the *adda* and those of modern civil society is understandable," Chakrabarty observes. "They are mutually antithetical organizations of time and place" (204). For that reason, the adda is disappearing (as is the printed book itself, one might say). In that sense, it is like the "subaltern" in being excluded from the logic of capitalist modernity, constituting "almost a zone of comfort in capitalism" (213). However, in Bengal itself, as Chakrabarty himself notes, the adda is a form of secular middle- or upper-class culture that depends for its identity on being separate from the cultural, and sometimes even the linguistic world of peasants, workers, the "poor," and, on the whole, with some notable exceptions, Bengali women.[7]

In other words, there is an acknowledged conflation in Chakrabarty's presentation of a national or regional "antithesis" represented by the adda or modern Bengali poetry (especially Tagore) within a formerly colonial and now a global capitalist order, with subalternity within a given national or regional context, like Bengal, where institutions like the adda or the Latin American literary tertulia are not "subaltern" at all but rather cultural formations proper in some ways to "the lettered city." That conflation may have something to do with the shifting nature of the relations between literature and power in modernity, and the question of literary bohemia in particular. But it may also have to do with the shift in the location of Chakrabarty and other South Asian subalternists from India to the U.S. academy, which makes the fault line of subalternity not so much one within Indian society and history as between Indian society and history and "Europe."[8]

For Chakrabarty, an institution like the adda and modern Bengali poetry generally are still grounded in a specific national or subnational regional context. Spivak, by contrast, makes a case for literature closer to Moreiras's own, that is, one that is postnational and cosmopolitan: *Death of a Discipline* reproduces a series of lectures she gave at the University of California, Irvine in 2000—before, that is, both 9/11 and the War on Terror, and the debate about "world literature" provoked by Franco Moretti and Pascale Casanova's *La République mondiale des lettres*. Globalization, Spivak observes, is said to undermine the traditional rationale for the study of literature and the humanities in general, founded on the relation of literature, national language, and the nation-state. Hence the idea of the "death" of her discipline, comparative literature, referred to in the title of her book: literature has lost its "modern" function of producing an ethically enlightened secular citizen-subject for the nation. Yet, Spivak responds, nothing is as challenging to the status quo today as literature. Literature is dead; long live literature. How can this be so?

Spivak explains that "what we are witnessing in the postcolonial and globalizing world is a return of the demographic, rather than territorial frontiers that predate and are larger than capitalism [and that] belonged to the shifting multicultural empires that preceded monopoly capitalism" (15). Literature and literary studies today, freed of their connection to the nation-state, potentially give us access to this new sense of territoriality and the residual or emerging collectivities that correspond to it. Spivak calls this possibility "planetarity," which she conceives of in antithesis to "globalization." Literature maintains precisely in its supplementarity a principle of resistance to capitalist rationalization based on a utilitarian, market-driven calculus:

> All around us is the claim for the rational destruction of the figure, the demand for not clarity but immediate comprehensibility by the ideological average. This destroys the force of literature as a cultural good. Anyone who believes that a literary education should still be sponsored by universities must allow that one must learn to read. And to learn to read is to learn to disfigure the undecidable figure into a responsible literality, again and again. . . . Literature is what escapes the system; you cannot speed read it. The figure "is" irreducible. (23)

Both Spivak and Chakrabarty lean at moments toward the traditional genre of "the defense of poetry." Moreiras, by contrast, is careful to differentiate his argument from the neo-Arielist assumption that literature and literary intellectuals as such are the privileged bearers of Latin America's cultural originality and possibility. That is because that assumption is one of the pillars of what Moreiras calls a "first-order"—or nationalist—Latin-americanism (literature is, so to speak, "lo nuestro" for a Latin American Latinamericanism). Yet Moreiras also shares Spivak's enthusiasm for literature as something that (to recall her own words) "escapes the system," seeing texts of modern Latin American art and literature—those he considers in *Tercer espacio*, for example—as forms of the political that transcend both the logic of neoliberal hegemony and a stunted and authoritarian (and ultimately unsuccessful) politics of the nationalist Left. That is because those texts perform at the same time a kind of deconstruction of rhetoric of identitarian claims that have become obsolete and suggest in their place new forms of identity and territoriality, akin to what Spivak means by "planetarity."

Like Spivak, Moreiras is attentive to the problem that "difference" has been or can be absorbed by what he understands as hegemony. Latin American alterity, in the various forms that Moreiras interrogates in *The Exhaustion of Difference*—which would include today, nearly a decade after the appearance of the book, some of the political forms of the marea rosada, like Chavismo or the Bolivian Movimiento al Socialismo (I will come back to this at the end of the chapter)—runs the risk of simply being incoporated into the logic of globalization, losing in the process whatever oppositional force it might have once had. Hanging most ominously over the pages of Moreiras's book is this threat of the cooptation or neutralization of difference, rather than its "exhaustion"—a threat similar in kind to the prospect of the historian's becoming an accomplice of domination that Walter Benjamin wrote about on the eve of the victory of fascism in Europe in his "Theses on the Philosophy of History." One can see the desire to combat that possibility of reactionary domestication—the conversion of Latin American alterity into a kind of postmodernist *costumbrismo*—in the work of deconstruction that Moreiras performs. And that "work of the negative," as he might put it, is in turn the basis for his claim that the work of deconstruction prepares the ground for a "transformative" politics. How should we judge that claim today?

Moreiras is not unaware of the problem that his work of "clearing" (to recall his own metaphor) may lead outside politics altogether. In *The Ex-*

haustion of Difference he appeals on this score to Spivak's "strategic essentialism," speaking of the possibility of a "double articulation" (questioning identity to the extent that it reifies domination, affirming identity when it is a question of struggling against domination). Moreiras is able on that basis to endorse at one point my own call for "a return to a strategic, nation-based populism as a means to reconstitute the possibility of a popular front alliance. A populist political strategy is not the same thing as a populist historicism" (320, n. 4). If I read this correctly, for Moreiras a kind of antifoundationalist populism, perhaps akin to (but not reducible to) what Laclau understands by "populist reason," is possible, at least in *The Exhaustion of Difference*, so long as it recognizes itself as "strategic"; that is, not "ontotheological," not essentialist. As we will see, however, he does not appear to either want or be able to sustain that claim.[9]

A somewhat different way of articulating "strategic essentialism" is to identify, explicitly or implicitly, the nature of Latin America itself, both as a historical experience and a project for the future, with deconstruction. Something like this is implicit in Moreiras's idea of "dirty atopianism" or "savage hybridity." Dirty atopianism, Moreiras explains, "is the name for a nonprogrammable program of thinking that refuses to find satisfaction in expropriating at the same time that it refuses to fall into appropriative drives" (23). "Savage hybridity" flows from this. As opposed to "cultural hybridity," where, as in Laclau's well-known formulation of "hegemonic articulation," a given cultural feature or artifact can be posited as an "empty signifier" for the "national" or collective as such, "savage hybridity is simply the recognition that every claim to totalization of identity, where the one is made to stand for the many, including the claim of hegemonic articulation itself, ultimately lacks foundation. . . . [A]s the 'other side' of the hegemonic relationship, savage hybridity preserves, or holds in reserve, the site of the subaltern, just as it preserves the site of a subalternist politics. It is not so much a locus of enunciation as it is an atopic site, not a place for ontopologies but a place for the destabilization of all ontopologies, for a critique of totality—*and* a place for the possibility of an *other* history" (294).

This is the moment where Moreiras comes, in my opinion, closest to proposing deconstruction itself as a new form of Latinamericanism. One sense of what this "atopian" place without place could mean is suggested by Moreiras in an essay that appeared prior to *The Exhaustion of Difference*:

CHAPTER THREE

Creo . . . que la reflexión latinoamericana o latinoamericanista está, por razones históricas y geopolíticas concretas, en una situación privilegiada. El cruce civilizacional latinoamericano, y su posición intermedia o vestibular en relación con los macroprocesos asociados con la globalización, otorgan a la Latinoamérica del presente un papel de encrucijada de la historia.[10]

[I think . . . that Latin American or Latinamericanist thinking is, for concrete historical and geopolitical reasons, in a privileged situation. The civilizational crisscross of Latin America and its intermediate or supplementary position in relation to the macroprocesses associated with globalization confer on the Latin America of today the role of a crossroads of history.]

Brett Levinson echoes Moreiras's image of the *encrucijada* as follows:

A criss-cross of worlds, Latin America is not itself reducible to a world, just as the meeting place of nation-states, to wit, the border, is irreducible to any such topos. And if Latin America is this embodiment — of the crossroads, of the West's *encrucijada* — then any Latin American identification with an actual cultural universe or location is necessarily the performance of the very alienation that the identification or appropriation is supposed to relieve.[11]

Moreiras and Levinson are concerned with maintaining what Moreiras calls the "irruptive" force of thought, as against the possibility of its commodification or reification. But it does not take much reflection to see reproduced here, as deconstruction, both the "appropriative," orientalizing gesture of a U.S. or Iberian-European Latinamericanism and the "restitutional excess" of a nationalist Latinamericanism (albeit now in the mode of something like Jean Luc Nancy's community-that-is-to-come rather than the historical nation). In a way, "savage hybridity" is not too different from the claim made by Alejo Carpentier, which Moreiras and Levinson would almost certainly distance themselves from, that the nature of Latin America is "baroque." In both cases — Latin America as "encrucijada" or atopia, Latin America as baroque — there is implicit a sense of the Latin American as a form of the *sublime*. We might say then that the deconstructive articulation of Latinamericanism falls short of its own promise, tending perilously close to a kind of tourist sublime, and does so, paradoxically, because of its own "affective investment" in its object of study.[12]

Moreiras, who is himself a non–Latin American Latinamericanist, is rightly skeptical of the neo-Arielist claim to epistemological, political, or ethical authority that is founded on being "in" or speaking "from" Latin America, as if there were not whole libraries in Latin America full of racist and reactionary literature, or of well-intentioned, but sometimes misguided (and sometimes racist too) progressive thought.[13] But, in truth, the location (in the sense of the "politics of location") of *The Exhaustion of Difference* is neither the conflicted tradition of Latin American cultural thought nor the Latinamericanism of the U.S. or Ibero-European academy and area studies: it is the space of cosmopolitan critical theory itself, which is itself produced by and feeds back into the logic of globalization. In this sense, though *The Exhaustion of Difference* registers the crisis of Latinamericanism brilliantly, it does not itself come out of that crisis; by contrast, the impulse behind both Latin American subaltern and cultural studies and the neo-Arielist response to these does. One might speak then of a relation of reverse dependency between deconstruction and a Latin American (subaltern) objective correlative that has been assigned the "atopian" task of being the concrete bearer of deconstruction. Would it be stretching the point to see the master-slave dialectic sneaking back in here, through the back door, so to speak?

That problem is compounded by what I think is a continuing overvaluation of intellectual and cultural critique that Moreiras and the New Latin Americanists share with neo-Arielism. Since its tools are those of philosophical critique, deconstruction is unable to interrogate adequately its own conditions of possibility; by contrast, I would see the essential (deconstructive?) impulse behind both subaltern studies and cultural studies as the displacement of the hermeneutic authority of the "traditional intellectual" (in Gramsci's sense of the term) and what traditional intellectuals consider authoritative cultural forms and practices, including written literature and "critique." What is not present in *The Exhaustion of Difference*, even as a registered absence, is the third component of Latinamericanism: that is, those forms of knowledge, culture, agency, and value that fit with neither metropolitan Latinamericanism nor a self-complacent Latin American Latinamericanism located essentially in Latin American urban middle- and upper-middle-class culture. It might be proper to call this a "subaltern" Latinamericanism, were it not for the fact that, as Moreiras himself notes, the idea is aporetic or self-contradictory, in the same way as the idea of "studying" the subaltern. Be that as it may, this "third" Latinamericanism could not be Moreiras's "third space" either—that is, the space of semiotic undecidability and (un)translatability itself. It is, rather, something more like what the Argentine philosopher Rudolfo Kusch understood by "popular thinking"—that is, a space of concrete quotidian struggles, informed by ideas about identity, history, self, and community that deconstruction would be obliged to find aporetic, if it is to remain true to its own ethics of knowledge (even to mention Kusch, of course, is from the point of view of deconstruction to raise the specter of "essentialism").[14] Deconstruction can march alongside these struggles and ideas—in this sense, Moreiras's claim of being on the side of the subaltern, like Spivak's, is not a specious one—but it cannot act in their place.

I would go one step further, however. The characteristic tropes of *The Exhaustion of Difference* and second-wave Latinamericanist deconstruction are post-dictatorship, trauma, mourning and melancholy, "inoperative community," "savage hybridity," the "remainder" or fragment, the ruin, the residue, the margin, allegory. That is no accident, because, as I noted earlier, the situation of the deconstructivist intervention in Latinamericanist discourse in both its first and second waves depends to some extent on the defeat of the historical Left in Latin America. It emerges—this is also the case of de Man and Derrida and deconstruction in the United States and France—in the place of a revolutionary project that had been volatized; and it remains in some ways fatally tied to that event. To the extent that the defeat of the Left was due to the inadequate or outmoded character of its discourse—and in particular the inadequacy of that discourse in the face of globalization and the collapse of communism—then deconstruction could (and did) serve as a place for revitalization. And to the extent that deconstruction is by definition a project of radical dedifferentiation, it could be said to be both in its theory and practice "anticipatory" in some sense of an egalitarian society. But with the resurgence of an actual political Left in Latin America, whatever its limitations might be, deconstruction can no longer command the strategic role it claimed for itself in the articulation of Latinamericanism, even as a critique of those limitations. It reveals itself instead as a form of melancholy that cannot detach itself from its conditions of possibility.

This unfruitful outcome of the encounter between deconstruction and Latinamericanism leads in two different and perhaps competing directions: On the one hand, towards a critique of political-cultural articulation as such and the embrace of a kind of procedural liberalism or "republicanism" (with lowercase *r*) in the mode of Hannah Arendt, who has become a more central presence in Moreiras's recent thought. If one had to specify what sort of politics is *immanent* to deconstruction (as opposed to the different political positions actually espoused by its practitioners, which can range from center-right to extreme left, but generally cluster around the center-left), it would be procedural liberalism, since that is the form of decision making that allows the ultimate ungroundedness or "infinitude of the social" to play itself out, without resulting in any totalitarian claim. It would be too much to say that Moreiras has moved explicitly into such a position; I think there is still in his thinking the desire for a "transformative" event. What is clear, however, is that he has moved well beyond the critique/reconstruction of Latinamericanism in *The Exhaustion of Difference* to question the "ontotheological" character of politics and political philosophy as such.[15]

The other direction, now reaching beyond deconstruction in what seems to be a Deleuzian fashion, is towards a kind of ultraleftism. That gesture involves something like a transference to (or a claim to find immanent in) the Latin American scene the agency of the "multitude" proposed by Hardt and Negri in *Empire*. Its most cogent expression has been the idea of a "posthegemonic" politics. Such a gesture is explicitly rooted in Moreiras's critique of hegemonic articulation, and in aspects of his idea of "savage hybridity," but it also claims to depart from Moreiras and second-wave deconstruction. As Jon Beasley-Murray, one of the most articulate exponents of "posthegemony," puts it:

> Where I differ from [Gareth] Williams and Moreiras is that I am not content with deconstruction, with posthegemony as permanent critique or labor of the negative. . . . The difference between hegemony theory and subaltern studies is simply that the political polarity is inverted: whereas Gramsci and Laclau would insist that politics is a matter of playing the game of hegemony, Spivak, Williams, and Moreiras question the rules of the game by pointing to the aporetic excess for which it can never account. But they seldom doubt the game itself. . . . By contrast, then, in my conception posthegemony goes beyond the wreckage of any hegemonic project. I aim to redescribe and reconstruct an image of society that no longer depends upon that society's own self portrayal.[16]

Beasley-Murray goes on in the same passage to invoke Negri on the multitude as a subject that "both pre-exists modern society . . . and returns in modernity's death throes."

Moreiras explicitly rejects Hardt's and Negri's invocation of the multitude, Agamben, Deleuze, and related arguments for an "immanentist" politics as a kind of naively humanist messianism, whose vision of a chiliastic outcome—the rule of the multitude—would have to be in turn deconstructed.[17] As my own remarks on Hardt and Negri in chapter 2 suggest, I share that skepticism. What is not clear, however, is what Moreiras would propose to put in the place of the "politics" of the multitude, but it is certainly not the marea rosada. Here, in an extended footnote in *Línea de sombra*, is his verdict on Evo Morales and the MAS government, at the moment of its accession to power in 2006:

> Hace apenas unos días que el nuevo presidente boliviano, Evo Morales Ayma, presentó su primer discurso presidencial, enfatizando las reivindicaciones indígenas en Bolivia, y ya han empezado a leerse bobadas en la prensa afirmando que Morales no es de izquierdas ni de derechas, pues estas son categorías de la tradición política europea con la que Morales no querría tener nada que ver. El propósito de Morales sería más bien la descolonización total de Tawantinsuyo como proyecto genuinamente indígena. Bien—más vale descolonizar que colonizar. Pero el éxito (deseable) de Morales será una función de la capacidad de su gobierno para fomentar la producción y redistribución de la riqueza y para crear la justicia social; no de la retórica, por lo demás tan respetable como cualquier otra, de Pachamama y ayllu. No es la descolonización infinita de lo cultural lo que más importa ni lo que más puede importar al pueblo boliviano, sino la justicia social y la capacidad republicana de la ciudadanía para obtener un sistema político y económico genuinamente democrático. El rechazo de la opresión cultural no es automáticamente traducible a la deseabilidad del desarrollo de una ciencia o de un derecho "propios." (*Línea*, 39, n. 9)

> [A few days ago the new president of Bolivia, Evo Morales Ayma, presented his first presidential speech, emphasizing indigenous demands in Bolivia, and already one reads in the press stupidities affirming that Morales is neither of the right or the left, since these are categories of European political tradition that Morales would prefer not to have anything to do with. Morales's proposal would be instead the total decolonization of the Tawantinsuyo as an authentically indigenous project. That is all well

and good — it is better to decolonize than to colonize. But the success (desired) of Morales will be a function of the ability of his government to encourage the production and redistribution of wealth and to create social justice; not of the rhetoric, which is in any case as respectable as any other, of Pachamama and ayllu. It is not the infinite decolonization of the cultural sphere that most matters nor should matter to the Bolivian people, but social justice and the republican capacity of the citizenry to obtain a genuinely democratic political and economic system. The rejection of cultural oppression does not automatically translate into the desirability of the development of an "autochthonous" science or law.]

I quote this passage at some length, because it seems to invoke the critique of the "restitutional excess" of identity politics proper to deconstruction as such and very much at the core of *The Exhaustion of Difference* in particular, here expanded into a critique of the "telluric-cultural" character of the postcolonial project as such, undoubtedly an allusion to the work of his former colleague at Duke University, Walter Mignolo; but at the same time it also sounds a new, distinctively Arendtian note — the appeal to "la capacidad republicana de la ciudadanía" — that is absent from the earlier book, where Moreiras is still grappling with the possibility of an "atopian" populist articulation that would not simply reproduce the "bad" populism of the Latin American past.

One wants to say in response to Moreiras: Yes, of course, any political project must justify itself by its results rather than its promises. And of course too, it is idiotic — a "bobada" — to say that the political position of Morales and the MAS is neither of the Right nor the Left, as if those categories were themselves a European imposition, derived from the accidental configuration of the chamber of deputies during the French Revolution. But without a "proyecto genuinamente indígena" — that is, without what Moreiras condescendingly dismisses as "la retórica . . . de Pachamama y ayllu" — there would be no possibility of political hegemony in the first place in a country like Bolivia, and without hegemony — that is, control of the state, and *from* the state of key institutions of civil society — there would be no possibility to "fomentar la producción y redistribución de la riqueza y para crear la justicia social." Moreover, what many people in Bolivia — probably the vast majority — might imagine as "social justice" today is precisely a recognition by and *in* the state and the state ideological apparatuses of languages and ways of thinking and being that have been suppressed or marginalized for centuries, not just by the Spanish colonial project, but also by successive forms of state "modernity" that have been built on the assumption of the inadequate or anachronistic character of indigenous life and culture. Moreiras is no doubt pointing to a kind of politics that would no longer be based on the friend/enemy distinction, and that would be genuinely transformative of what we can be as human beings. But to get to that point, a more conventional politics of some sort is necessary. *After* apartheid, "forgiveness," multilateralism, Derrida's "politics of friendship" are possible in South Africa, even necessary to ground a new form of national-popular hegemony; but to end apartheid required a *struggle*, both political and military.

As for the comment about a "rhetoric . . . as respectable [*tan respetable*] as any other," that is, of course, the scorn of the philosopher for the demagogue, of Plato for the Sophists. But is it in fact true to say that the rhetoric of the Master Race and the Final Solution is "as respectable" as "the rhetoric . . . of Pachamama and ayllu"? Moreiras confuses here, in a way that I think is fatal for his position, the *form* of ideology—what Althusser called "Ideology in General"—with the *content* of particular ideologies.[18]

It seems, then, that *both* of these distinct (albeit related) outcomes to the unexpected impasse deconstruction encounters in its pretended relation with Latinamericanism—that is, Moreiras's critique of the "onto-theological" character of politics and the apocalyptic ultraleftism of the "multitude" and "posthegemony"—involve in fact a *renunciation* of actual politics, which means that despite their claim to be "transformative," they remain complicit with the existing order of things.

I will come back to this point, and to the question of the relation of subalternism, deconstruction, and hegemony in relation to the Bolivian case in particular in the final chapter.

Between Ariel and Caliban:
The Politics of Location of Latinamericanism
and the Question of Solidarity

In a wonderful essay called "Académicos y *gringos malos*" on five auto-biographical or semi-autobiographical novels by Latin American writers that center on their experiences in U.S. universities, Fernando Reati and Gilberto Gómez Ocampo register the articulation of what they coincide with me in calling a "neo-Arielist" position: that is, a reassertion of the authority of literature, literary criticism, and literary intellectuals as the bearers of Latin America's cultural memory and possibility against insti-tutions and forms of thought and experience identified with the United States—in this case departments of Spanish or writing programs at mainly Midwestern universities. They see that position as entailing a kind of pre-mature foreclosure—an "imperialismo al revés" in the phrase of one of the novelists—based on an anxiety about loss of identity:

> En todos los [cinco] casos, el choque inicial con la cultura norteameri-cana afirma de modo casi instantáneo la identidad latinoamericana de los protagonistas, y salir—huir—de Estados Unidos para retornar a América Latina se impone como condición para ganar una perspectiva crítica que les permita producir una imagen opuesta a los clichés y estereotipos contra cuales reaccionan. No es de sorprender entonces que varias novelas coin-cidan en finales que enfatizan un sentido de cierre más que de apertura hacia lo nuevo aprendido.[1]

> [In each of the [five] cases, the initial clash with North American culture affirms almost instantaneously the Latin American identity of the protago-

nists, and leaving—fleeing—the United States to return to Latin America imposes itself as the condition for gaining a critical perspective that permits them to produce an image opposed to the clichés and stereotypes against which they are reacting. It is no surprise then that several of these novels have endings that emphasize a sense of closure more than of opening toward the newly learned.]

I want to use Reati's and Goméz Ocampo's remarks to try to map the "politics of location" of Latinamericanism and my own place as an academic and a "gringo bueno" in them. I rely here, as elsewhere in this book, on Nelly Richard's distinction of critical theory written "desde/sobre Latinoamérica," from or about Latin America.[2] I will start by noting what seems at first sight a paradoxical coincidence between the terms of David Stoll's much publicized attack on Rigoberta Menchú and various critiques by Latin American literary intellectuals of the pertinence of what might be called in a kind of shorthand "studies" (cultural, postcolonial, subaltern, ethnic, queer, latino, africana, et cetera) to the field, or endeavor, of Latin America's knowledge about itself. To connect this chapter with the previous one, I should note that these critiques are also sometimes directed against the convergence of Latinamericanism and deconstruction proposed by Moreiras and the New Latin Americanism, to the extent that deconstruction is seen as a discourse "about" rather than "from" Latin America. But at other times, as in the case of Richard herself, they represent a specifically Latin American articulation of deconstruction concerned to dismantle the assumptions of a European or U.S.-based academic Latinamericanism.

Stoll's argument was not only or perhaps even mainly with Menchú, or about whether several key details of her narrative were factually true, but rather was directed against what he perceived as the hegemony of the discourses of postmodernism and multiculturalism in the North American academy, which, in his view, consciously or unconsciously colluded to perpetuate international support for armed struggle in Guatemala by promoting *I, Rigoberta Menchú* and making Menchú into an icon of political correctness. The connection between multiculturalism and postmodernism that troubled Stoll is predicated on the fact that multiculturalism carries with it what, in a well-known essay, the Canadian philosopher Charles Taylor called a "presumption of equal worth."[3] That presumption implies a demand for epistemological relativism that coincides with the postmodernist critique of the Enlightenment paradigm of modernity—what Habermas would call communicative rationality. If there is no one universal standard for truth, then claims about truth are contextual: they have to do with how people construct different understandings of the world and historical memory from the same set of facts in situations of gender, ethnic, and class inequality, exploitation, and repression. The truth claims for a narrative like *I, Rigoberta Menchú* depend on conferring on testimonio a special kind of epistemological authority embodying subaltern experience and "voice." But, for Stoll—who was arguing also against the emergence of what he called a "postmodernist anthropology"—this amounts to an idealization of the quotidian realities of peasant life to favor the prejudices of a metropolitan academic audience, in the interest of a solidarity politics that (in his view) did more harm than good. Against the authority of testimonial voice, Stoll wanted to affirm the authority of the fact-gathering procedures of traditional anthropology or journalism, in which accounts like Menchú's would be treated simply as raw material that must be processed by more objective techniques of assessment.

The argument *from* Latin America—"desde Latinoamérica"—against "studies" has three major components:

1. "Studies" represents a North American problematic about identity politics and multiculturalism, and/or a historically recent British Commonwealth problematic about decolonization, that have been displaced onto Latin America at the expense of misrepresenting its quite diverse histories and social-cultural formations, which are not easily reducible to either multiculturalism or postcoloniality.

2. The prestige of "studies" as a discourse formation emanating from and sustained by the resources of the Euro–North American academy occludes the prior engagement by Latin American intellectuals—"on native grounds," so to speak—with the very questions of historical and cultural representation they are concerned with. That prestige portends, therefore, an overt or tacit negation of the status and authority of Latin American intellectuals, a willful forgetting of what Hugo Achúgar calls "el pensamiento latinoamericano." The new hegemony of metropolitan theoretical models amounts in Latin America to a kind of cultural neocolonialism, concerned with the brokering by the North American and European academy of knowledge from and about Latin America. In this transaction, the Latin American

intellectual is relegated to the status of an *object* of theory (as subaltern, postcolonial, Calibanesque, etc.), rather than its *subject*.

3. By foregrounding the theme of the incommensurability of subaltern or marginalized social subjects and the nation-state, postcolonial and subaltern studies contribute to diminishing Latin America's ability to implement its own projects of national or regional identity and development. Beyond an appeal to the agency of an abjected, precapitalist or premodern other that remains outside of (any possible) hegemonic representation, "studies" lacks a sense of the political as grounded in a local, national, and regional public sphere, the continuity of the nation, a more or less active and politically informed citizenry, local memory, and projects that seek to affirm the interests of both individual Latin American nation-states and Latin America as a whole in globalization.[4]

Both Stoll and the neo-Arielist critics of "studies" coincide in seeing the discourses of U.S. multiculturalism and postmodernist relativism as the main culprits. They also both, in some ways, attempt to police their respective disciplinary fields (anthropology and literary criticism) against their destabilization by new forms of interdisciplinarity like cultural studies, and the impact developments in those fields might have on the larger public sphere. As such, there is a tendency for them to pass over into neoconservatism. (I will take up the question of neoconservatism, which must be distinguished from conservatism pure and simple, on the one hand, and from neoliberalism, on the other, at length in chapter 5.)

What complicates the identification of Stoll and Latin American critics of "studies," however, is the fact that Stoll is a North American writing about a Latin American organic intellectual—Rigoberta Menchú—whereas the Latin American neo-Arielists are critiquing what they see as a new North American academic fashion—"el *boom* del subalterno," in Mabel Moraña's telling phrase. Here, within what on the surface might seem a shared critique of postmodernist relativism and multiculturalism, a different cutting edge comes into play, one that takes us back to the Ariel-Caliban polarity, except that now Rigoberta Menchú is in the place of Ariel, facing the power and vulgarity of the Colossus of the North, "the triumph of Caliban" in Rubén Darío's image, represented by Stoll.

In contrast to the "imperialism in reverse" of the five Latin American academic novels analyzed by Reati and Goméz Ocampo, there is a "national allegory"—to borrow Fredric Jameson's useful term—that is about U.S. imperialism pure and simple that I think is worth introducing here. It is Richard Harding Davis's novel *Soldiers of Fortune*, which at the time of its publication in 1897 became something of a bestseller and fed the public enthusiasm in the United States for intervention in Cuba. *Soldiers of Fortune* (which bears an obvious debt to Conrad's *Nostromo*), is set in the fictional Latin American republic of Olancho, recognizably Venezuela, where, as it happens, I was born (my father worked for a subsidiary, Creole Petroleum, of what was later to become Exxon). The hero, Robert Clay, is a civil engineer who is hired by Langham, the owner of Valencia Mining Company, to manage his iron mines in Olancho. Langham's concession depends on a contract negotiated with the president of Olancho, a Señor Alvarez, which provides the Olanchan government with a 10 percent share of production. The nationalist opposition to Alvarez in the Olanchan senate, led by General Mendoza, objects to the concession, and introduces legislation to obtain a larger share of the mine's production. In a kind of Machiavellian double-cross, Clay meets secretly with Mendoza and offers him a huge bribe to block this legislation, which Mendoza accepts. Clay then reneges on the bribe, threatening at the same time to make public Mendoza's acquiescence in his plot. Mendoza responds by preparing a coup d'état to overthrow Alvarez and nationalize the mines. He puts into circulation the rumor that President Alvarez is a dupe of foreign interests, namely the Valencia Mining Company, Alvarez's wife (who is Spanish, and who Mendoza claims is plotting to restore the Spanish monarchy in Olancho), and Alvarez's chief of security, Stuart, who is a British subject. Mendoza also enlists in his plot a shadowy figure called Captain Burke, a gringo arms smuggler and *filibustero*, on the model of William Walker (Burke also anticipates in some ways the character of Mr. Danger in Rómulo Gallegos's *Doña Bárbara*, one of the best-known examples of the figure of the *gringo malo* or Ugly American in Latin American fiction).

Clay and Stuart get wind of Mendoza's plans and find out in particular that Burke has smuggled in a shipment of weapons for the plotters. Clay, who has won the loyalty of the Olanchan mine workers, organizes them into a kind of Contra army *avant la lettre*. They locate the smuggled arms and capture them. This precipitates Mendoza's coup, which is initially successful: Mendoza captures the Presidential Palace and imprisons Alvarez. A sector of the army, however, remains loyal to Alvarez's vice president, Rojas. They put themselves under the command of Clay, whom they designate the Liberator of Olancho. Mendoza's coup collapses and he is eventually shot to death in combat. In due time, the United States Marines arrive. Clay directs them to preserve order until Rojas can be installed as the new president of Olancho. Rojas, it goes without saying, pledges to recognize the virtues of free trade and protect the security of the Valencia Mining Company.

At the beginning of the novel, Clay is engaged to Langham's older daughter, Alice. Alice and her younger sister, Hope, come to visit Olancho on the eve of Mendoza's coup. Alice is the archetypal North American upper-class genteel woman: elegant, refined, ultrafeminine, educated according to European models. She seems an ideal match for Clay, who is clearly the man who will inherit the place of her father. In Olancho, however, the two come to regard each other differently. Escaping from an ambush by Mendoza's forces, Alice sees Clay working with his hands to try to repair a ship engine. The experience convinces her that his experience and his values are at odds with her own. Like the nationalist opposition in the Olanchan senate, her values are anachronistic: they represent an older North American bourgeois culture that is being displaced by the dynamic new forces of corporate imperialism. By contrast, Alice's sister, Hope, epitomizes precisely these new forces. She is only eighteen, and has not come out into society. Her very youth and naiveté permit her to be open to the new, since she is as yet uncorrupted by inherited privilege, represented on the one hand by her sheltered upbringing in New York, on the other by the oligarchy in Olancho, whose carefully coded distinctions of status she ignores. She is a more suitable match for Clay than Alice because her values are, like his, democratic, egalitarian, and pragmatic. Unlike her sister, she is a figure of a feminine modernity: energetic, self-motivated, physically active, androgynous, in the novel's own words, "like a boy."

Hope, like Rojas and the Olanchan mine workers—and it is significant that it is the workers and not the elite who choose to side with Clay against Mendoza—symbolize the advantages of an alliance with the emerging forms of American imperial power, involving a remapping of older national and regional loyalties and values, a remapping that is also Clay's raison d'être, and which requires the displacement of the traditional elites in both the United States and Latin America.

The libidinal economy allegorized in the Clay-Alice-Hope relation serves as a "foundational fiction" in Doris Sommer's sense of this term, here not so much for the nation as for the emerging supranational territoriality of corporate imperialism that follows with the close of the western frontier in the United States. It goes without saying that although this territoriality is supranational, the values that govern its identity remain in some significant sense North American: the triumph of those values, which the plot of the novel enacts, symbolizes the hegemonization of the Latin American imaginary by U.S. culture and values. The contemporary equivalent of *Soldiers of Fortune* would be a text "from" Latin America like Jorge Volpi's *El insomnio de Bolívar*, which, as I noted in the introduction, argues essentially for Latin America's incorporation by the United States.

Figuratively, Clay-Hope, and their alliance with a new Latin American subject represented by Rojas and the miners, could be read as a figure for "studies." "Studies," like Clay-Hope, speaks the language of democracy, anti-elitism, the popular, the subaltern, and the new; but (in the eyes of many Latin American intellectuals) it remains at the service of U.S. global and regional hegemony, and it does so in the name of a posture of benevolent solidarity. By the same token, however, the resistance to "studies" "desde América Latina" must be figured as Mendoza and the nationalist opposition, that is, as a reactionary (or, perhaps more generously, a reactive) position.

Let me be clear, because the possibilities for misunderstanding are rife here. There can be no question that the main enemy of democracy in Latin America has been U.S. hegemony over the region — time and again democratically elected regimes have been overthrown with U.S. support or connivance, the last, now shamefully with Obama's acquiescence if not approval, being the coup d'état in Honduras in 2009. But the obstacles to democracy and social equality are also *internal* to Latin American nation-states; indeed, as in the case of the Honduran coup, it is often those internal barriers — invariably tied to forms of racial and class privilege — that U.S. policy has used historically to destabilize the Left and democratic regimes.

I believe that the things that divide "studies" from its neo-Arielist critics in Latin America are less important in the long run than the concerns we share. I am sensitive in particular to the concern with the prestige and power of the North American academy in an era in which Latin American universities and intellectual life have been decimated by neoliberal policies connected in great measure to U.S. hegemony over the region. If in fact globalization entails a displacement of the authority of Latin American intellectuals, then the resistance to "studies" must itself be ex-

CHAPTER FOUR

pressive in some way of the *unequal* position of Latin American culture, states, economies, and intellectual work in the current world system. Paul de Man memorably described the resistance to theory as itself theory. So there must also be a kind of "theory"—or "theoretical babbling," to use Hugo Achúgar's expression—inherent in the neo-Arielist position.[5]

But Arielism by definition is an ideologeme of what José Joaquín Brunner once called the "'cultured' vision of culture": that is, the vision that identifies culture essentially with high culture. For it is not only "in theory" (cultural, subalternist, postcolonial, Marxist and post-Marxist, feminist, queer, or the like), or from the metropolitan academy, that the authority of the Latin American "lettered city" is being challenged. This is also a consequence of the effects of globalization and the new social movements inside Latin America itself. Subaltern studies shares with cultural studies—this is the main point of convergence between the two projects—a sense that cultural democratization implies a shift of hermeneutic authority from the philological-critical activity of the "lettered city" to popular reception, a shift that entails a corresponding displacement of the authority of what Gramsci called the traditional intellectual (and literary intellectuals are, along with priests or clergy, almost paradigmatically traditional intellectuals).

The problem, of course, is that the displacement of the Latin American intellectual occurs not only "from below" but also from the right, so to speak, as neoliberal policies have restructured the Latin American university and secondary education system, and revalorized what counts as significant academic or professional credentials in a way that devalued literary or humanistic knowledge. One can understand neo-Arielism in these terms as a reaction to the authority of U.S. culture and the pernicious effects of U.S. hegemony on Latin American intellectual and cultural life, just as Rodó's *Ariel*, or Rubén Darío's "La entronización de Calibán" with its almost Brechtian image of North Americans as "búfalos de dientes de plata," or José Martí's "Nuestra América" were models of resistance to Anglo-American values at the end of the nineteenth century. But by rejecting explicitly or implicitly the validity of forms of sociocultural difference and antagonism based on popular-subaltern positions *in* Latin America, the neo-Arielist argument against "studies" may also entail a kind of unconscious *blanqueamiento*, which misrepresents the history and demographic heterogeneity of even those countries it claims to speak for.

Michael Aronna's argument that Rodó's construction of the Ariel/Caliban binary involves not only the opposition to the United States, but also class anxiety and something like what Eve Kosofsky Sedgwick meant by "homosexual panic," seems pertinent in this respect:

> Rodó retained the sexually degenerate characterization of Caliban, which is inextricably tied into the gendered, biological denigration of the indigenous populations. . . . The suggestion of Caliban's ethnic and sexual enervation is also indicated by intimations of sexual deviancy within democracy. . . . Rodó refers to egalitarian democracy as a "*zoocracia.*" . . . Rodó's vision of Caliban also borrows from Ernest Renan's reactionary and racist version of *The Tempest, Caliban, suite de La Tempete* (1878). In this work Renan condemns the Commune of 1870 as the product of a congenitally and sexually degenerate working class. . . . The concept of an uncontrollable and unjust national uprising led by supposedly "inferior" elements of society, the Calibans and their "barbarie vencedora," clearly reproduces the nineteenth-century Latin American discourse of civilization versus barbarism. . . . Rodó links his proposal for pan-American regeneration to a sensually charged yet rigidly chaste masculine enclave of learning and introspection. . . . Yet the therapeutic program proposed in *Ariel* is plagued by anxiety concerning the potential for excessive self-absorption and homosexuality within Rodó's idealized and repressed vision of male bonding.[6]

Aronna's characterization is, of course, historically specific to Rodó and his contemporaries, who represent a certain moment of bourgeois nationalism in Latin America, and not to today's neo-Arielists, who more often than not identify explicitly with the Left. Yet by asserting the authority of a prior Latin American literary-intellectual tradition and by identifying that tradition with the affirmation of national or regional identity against a foreign other, the United States, seen as a semibarbarous Caliban (or an authoritarian Prospero, who seeks to profit from both Ariel and Caliban), the neo-Arielist resistance to "studies" undercuts its own argument in a way. In order to defend the unity and integrity of individual Latin American nations and of Latin America itself against their resubordination in the emerging global system, the neo-Arielists are forced to put aside some of the relations of exclusion and inclusion, subordination and domination that operate *within* the frame of those nations and what counts as their "national" cultures. But the questions posed by those relations—in some cases questions they themselves raised in their work—are crucial in rethinking and reformulating the political project of the Latin American Left in conditions of globalization.

We arrive in this fashion at the following impasse. The new forms of theory emanating especially from the U.S. academy in the 1980s and 1990s—that is, what I am calling "studies"—may find allies in Latin America, but, as in the case of Clay in *Soldiers of Fortune*, only at the expense of destabilizing (or, perhaps more to the point, being accused of destabilizing) a prior progressive-nationalist Latin American tradition of critical thought. "Studies" runs the risk in this sense of constituting, unwillingly perhaps, but effectively, a new kind of pan-Americanism, now located in the humanities as opposed to the social sciences (the core of area studies), in which, in the mode of Santí's variation on Said's construction of Orientalism, metropolitan knowledge centers work out *their* problem in "knowing" and representing Latin America. One might argue in response that the point of "studies" in the first place was not to contribute to expanding U.S. hegemony over Latin America but rather to open up a new understanding and possibility of solidarity with forms of popular agency and resistance in Latin America. However, it is that very claim of solidarity that is contested by the neo-Arielist position.[7]

The prior Latin American tradition displaced in the name of egalitarianism by "studies" may reassert or reinvent itself against the influence of "studies," but it does so at the expense of reaffirming exclusions and hierarchies of value and privilege that are internal to Latin America and that represent carryovers into modernity of colonial and postcolonial forms of racial, ethnic, class, and gender discrimination. In this sense, the resistance to "studies," although it is undertaken in the name of the project of the Latin American Left, creates a barrier to fulfilling one of the key goals of that very project, which is the democratization of the Latin American subject and field of culture. That is because what is at stake in this project is inverting the hierarchical relation between a cultural-political elite, constituted as such in part by its possession of the power of writing and literature, and the "people," constituted as such in part by illiteracy or partial literacy or otherwise limited access to the forms of bourgeois high culture.

U.S. Latino critical thought might seem to point to a way beyond this impasse, to the extent that it could be said to be located "between" the Latin American and the North American, Ariel and Caliban, or Prospero and Ariel/Caliban. But as of yet it has not. If it seeks a genealogy for itself in a prior tradition of Latin American literature and cultural thought, as José David Saldívar tried to do in one of the foundational texts of Latino studies, *The Dialectics of Our America*, then, like the neo-Arielists, it re-inscribes the authority of the "lettered city" and its characteristic high-culture ideologemes: *mundonovismo*, "la raza cósmica," indigenism, mestizaje, magic realism, transculturation, the baroque and neobaroque, and now perhaps "hybridity." If, in the mode of "studies," it gestures at assimilating instead the values of U.S. Latino popular and mass culture against what is seen as an exhausted and in some ways irrelevant Latin American literary tradition it risks becoming an essentially affirmative discourse of U.S. exceptionalism.[8] In fact, some neo-Arielists—I am thinking again of Hugo Achúgar—argue that U.S. Latino culture is not part of Latin American culture, that it responds rather to the urgencies of U.S. civil society and to the needs of Latin American immigrants to naturalize themselves as U.S. subjects.

What is at issue here is not the correctness of arguments on one side or the other, but the fact itself of a polarization between the United States and Latin America and the charged affective fields that it sets up. Recalling a point made by Marx in the preface to *A Contribution to the Critique of Political Economy*, this polarization is "independent of our wills." It is not subject to argument or "dialogue," in other words. The question remains, then: Is it still possible to do cultural criticism from the U.S. academy "sobre Latinoamerica" that is in solidarity with the cause of Latin America and that is not, in some sense or other, Orientalist? In other words, is a progressive form of Latin American studies still possible? Like Latino criticism, a U.S. (or Western European) Latinamericanism also seems to be caught in a bind: to the extent that it seeks to be something like an academic version of the "preferential option for the poor" of liberation theology, its ethical, political, and epistemological impulse is to destabilize the field of area studies, including Latin American studies, as such. As in the case of Clay and the Olanchan mine workers, there is a possibility of solidarity between "studies" and the Latin American subaltern, but it is at the expense of solidarity with the resistance of Latin America to U.S. domination. On the other hand, the possibility of solidarity with the agendas of Latin American regional and national interests seems to preclude the possibility of solidarity—via "studies"—with the Latin American subaltern: that is, the workers, peasants, women, *indios*, blacks, subproletarians, street children, prostitutes, *descamisados, rotos, cabezas negras, cholos*, who are subaltern in part precisely because they are not adequately represented by the values and agendas of the "lettered city."

Does the identification of "studies" with a Latin American subaltern or popular subject preclude then the possibility of its solidarity with the new, explicitly nationalist projects of the Latin American marea rosada in particular? Speaking for myself, that is, from the position of a "gringo bueno" who saw his critical work as linked to solidarity politics, what all this means is that the terrain of Latinamericanism as a discourse formation "sobre Latinoamérica" has become slippery and ambiguous. During the Cold War, one could say that the terrain of Latin American studies was *contested*, but it was—or at least seemed—solid. To the extent that it was more than an ethical impulse, the possibility of solidarity rested on the recognition of a synergy between the fortunes of the Euro–North American Left and the Latin American Left, a sense that the fates of both were, for better or worse, connected. To deny the possibility or the desirability of solidarity, which is the point of coincidence between Stoll and neo-Arielism, amounts to saying that this is no longer the case, if, indeed, it was anything more than a benevolently paternalistic illusion in the first place.

I am remembering as I say this Foucault's remark about the embarrassment of speaking for others. I am tempted to conclude that the time has come for me personally to take a certain distance from Latinamericanism, a distance that would be marked, as my national allegory suggests, by a conscious reinvestment in my own problematic and always deferred identification with the United States.

But things could not be as simple as that. That is so in part because of my own personal circumstances.[9] But it is also so because of the very logic of wanting to move into a U.S. frame, for if one wants to speak of the political and cultural future of the United States, then, as I argue throughout these chapters, it seems to me clear that Latin America has become a crucial dimension of that future. What would it mean then to pose the question of the United States "desde Latinoamérica"—that is, from my own investment in Latin America and Latin American radical politics and criticism—instead of, as I have been doing for so many years, posing the question of Latin America *from* the United States?

The Neoconservative Turn

We are in the midst of something like a neoconservative "turn" in recent Latin American literary and cultural criticism. This phenomenon is doubly paradoxical: first, because it occurs in the context of the re-emergence of the Latin American Left as a political force in the period since 9/11; second, because the turn itself comes principally *from* the Left. The latter consideration is not an entirely new one, of course: it was also the case of Borges and Octavio Paz in previous generations, for example (I will come back to the question of Borges and his role as a signifier of Latinamericanism at the end of the chapter). The neoconservative turn has roots in both the deconstructive and the neo-Arielist articulations of Latinamericanism I discussed previously here. But it also endeavors to create a kind of space for itself.

I will consider three texts that I think are representative of the neoconservative turn: *La articulación de las diferencias* by the Guatemalan writer Mario Roberto Morales, published originally in 1998, with a second edition in 2002; Mabel Moraña's essay "Borges y yo: Primera reflexión sobre 'El etnógrafo'"; and (in somewhat greater detail) Beatriz Sarlo's book on Argentine testimonios of the period of Dirty War, *Tiempo pasado* (2005).[1]

Before moving on, it might be useful to pause briefly to distinguish between neoconservatism and neoliberalism, particularly since these positions are often blurred in actual forms of right-wing hegemony, like the Pinochet dictatorship in Chile, or Uribe in Colombia and the Partido Acción Nacional (PAN) government in Mexico today. Neoliberals believe in the efficacy of the free market and a utilitarian, rational-choice model of human agency, based on a maximization of gain and minimization of loss. In principle, neoliberalism does not propose any a priori hierarchy of value other than the existence of consumer desire as such and the effectiveness of the market and formal democracy as mechanisms for exercising free choice. For those purposes, it is just as well if you prefer pop culture to high culture, salsa to Schoenberg. The dehierarchization implicit in neoliberal theory and policy also entails, therefore, a strong challenge to the authority of intellectual elites in determining standards of cultural value and carrying out cultural critique. Neoconservatives, by contrast, believe there is a hierarchy of values embedded in "Western Civilization" and in the academic disciplines—a hierarchy essentially grounded in the Enlightenment paradigm—which it is important to defend and impart pedagogically and critically. That role requires the activity and authority of traditional intellectuals, in the sense that Gramsci used this term (that is, intellectuals who speak *as* intellectuals in the name of the universal), operating through religion, the university and education system, and in the war of ideas of the public sphere. In extreme cases, such as the one represented in the U.S. academy by Leo Strauss and his disciples, many of whom had important roles in both the Bush administrations, some neoconservative intellectuals are skeptical about democracy itself and the ability of the masses to effectively make choices and govern themselves. They argue for the preservation of a façade of formal democracy, but for de facto rule by an educated elite. Neoconservatives favor the humanities, especially the fields of philosophy and literature. Economics, by contrast, is the model discipline for neoliberals.

For purposes of illustration, we could say that, in a Latin American context, the Vargas Llosas (father and son), or the so-called McOndo writers anthologized by Alberto Fuguet, or the Mexican Generación Crack (and especially Jorge Volpi), or the tendency in cultural studies that puts a primary emphasis on consumer choice and "civil society," represent an implicit or explicit acceptance of a neoliberal position. But those—and related—tendencies are something quite different from what I mean here by the neoconservative turn. In fact, in some ways the neoconservative turn in Latin America is directed precisely *against* such tendencies in cultural production and theory, which dominated the scene in the previous period. To use Raymond Williams's useful distinction, neoliberalism is the *residual* tendency and neoconservativism is, or is bidding to be, the *emergent* tendency in Latin American cultural and literary studies. And it arises precisely at a juncture in which neoliberalism is losing to some extent its hegemony as an ideology among sectors of the regional and global bourgeoisie and professional classes (I will come back to this point).[2]

My ironic suggestion above of the dichotomy salsa/Schoenberg, to represent the difference between neoliberal and neoconservative positions, may strike some readers as facetious. It alludes to Theodor Adorno's famous juxtaposition of Stravinsky and Schoenberg in *The Philosophy of Modern Music*. I mean it to invoke the link between left-modernist aesthetic theory, especially as developed by Adorno and the Frankfurt school, and aspects of the neoconservative turn in the United States. For Adorno, Schoenberg's cultivation of dissonance and the twelve-tone composition method represented, as Kafka or Beckett did in literature, the force of an aesthetic modernism capable of blasting open, if only for a moment, a dominant capitalist culture based on commodity fetishism and consumer gratification. Stravinsky, by contrast, represented in his compositional methods what Fredric Jameson calls, in his essay on postmodernism, "pastiche" (what Adorno says about Stravinsky provides the template for Jameson's description of postmodernism). For Adorno, the critical, antihegemonic force of culture lies in a notion of aesthetic force and value that is not subject to consumer choice.

If figures like Herbert Marcuse represented a left-wing articulation of Frankfurt school "cultural critique" in the 1960s, there was also a more culturally conservative elaboration, which took place particularly within the group known as the New York Intellectuals, generally Trotskyist or social democratic in orientation, like Daniel Bell, who had interacted with Frankfurt school scholars during their period of exile in the United States. The key text in that regard may have been Bell's *The Cultural Contradictions of Capitalism*, which identified a growing split between the highly Oedipalized character structure necessary for capitalist production, and the narcissistic, pleasure-oriented character structure elicited by capitalist consumer culture. That distinction, which was also for Bell a distinction between "modern" and "postmodern" cultural regimes, allowed Bell, who himself came from a social democratic background, to claim, famously, that he was a liberal in economic policy but a conservative in cultural matters. Some of the earliest forms of neoconservatism in the United States emerge in the early 1970s in the work of art critics such as Clement Greenburg or Hilton Kramer as a reaction to the radicalism of sixties counterculture and as a defense of aesthetic modernism, represented for them in U.S. art by the heritage of abstract expressionism rejected by the Pop artists and the minimalists.[3]

This unexpected nexus in the early history of U.S. neoconservatism—or a certain aspect of it—between an initial "left" or left-liberal position and a right-wing political evolution seems to me particularly interesting, and troubling, for the present conjuncture. That is because the neoconservative turn in Latin America can and does represent itself, powerfully, as a position that comes from the Left and is still active within it. The neoconservative turn in the United States was a major factor in splitting both the New Left and the Democratic Party in the 1970s, partly along generational, racial, and ethnic lines. In that way, it inhibited the formation of the new, popular-democratic historical bloc in U.S. political culture that might have come out of the sixties, and it helped pave the way for the conservative restoration under Reagan. If I am correct in my diagnosis of a neoconservative turn in Latin American criticism, my concern is that it may similarly act to inhibit or limit the Latin American Left's goals and possibilities in the coming period.

With this in mind, let me turn to the three texts I have chosen to illustrate the neoconservative turn, beginning with Mario Roberto Morales's *La articulación de las diferencias*.[4] Morales centers his analysis on the so-called *debate interétnico* that developed in the wake of the 1996 signing of the peace accords between the guerrillas and the government in Guatemala, a debate he participated in himself as a columnist for the Guatemalan newspaper *Siglo Veintiuno*. One of his main concerns in his book is with the way in which Rigoberta Menchú and her famous testimonio were canonized in the U.S. academy by "politically correct" scholars like myself in the name of the "subaltern," or multiculturalism. He shares that concern with David Stoll in his well-known polemic against Menchú;[5] but unlike Stoll, who intended his book as a critique of what he called "postmodernist" tendencies in the social sciences in the U.S. academy, Morales is more concerned with the effects *within* Guatemala of the academic canonization of Menchú, which, he feels, are to legitimize the emergent discourses (in the 1990s) of pan-Mayan cultural nationalism and identity politics.

Morales's way of posing the problem of Mayan cultural nationalism stems from a double crisis that crosses his own person: the crisis of the Central American revolutionary Left, which he was active in; and the crisis of the concept of the writer as a sort of literary Moses, a "conductor de pueblos," to borrow Hernán Vidal's phrase, which was deeply embedded in the cultural practices of the Latin American Left in the sixties and seventies.[6] The idea of a synergistic relation between literature and national liberation struggle found its most powerful expression perhaps in Ángel Rama's concept of "transculturación narrativa."[7] Although the idea of transculturation comes from cultural anthropology, and the work of Fernando Ortiz in particular, for Rama, narrative transculturation was something that happened paradigmatically in literature. The Latin American boom novel in particular allowed in his view for the representation of a cultural *teleology* of the national, not without moments of violence, conflict, cultural (and actual) genocide, adaptation, or tenacious resistance, but *necessary* (or inevitable) in the last instance for the formation of inclusive national-popular cultures in Latin America, and corresponding modern nation-states. Transculturation was meant to be the cultural or superstructural correlative of the process of economic "delinking" and autonomous national development and modernization advocated by dependency theory.

Morales in effect revives Rama's idea of narrative transculturation, but now in the newly fashionable idiom of cultural studies and hybridity— *La articulación de las diferencias* could be read in some ways as a Guatemalan or "glocal" version of Néstor García Canclini's *Culturas híbridas*, although it retains a stress on literature in a way that Canclini does not. Morales concedes that texts like *I, Rigoberta Menchú* and the emerging discourses of Mayan identity politics are born out of conditions of extreme poverty and oppression in a deeply racist neocolonial society, and more immediately out of the trauma of the so-called Mayan Holocaust represented by the counterinsurgency campaign of the Guatemalan army in the early 1980s.[8] Nevertheless, Morales feels they tend to "essentialize" indigenous identity. Rather than an authentic multicultural democratization of Guatemalan society, he argues, Mayan identity politics propose in effect a negotiation between indigenous elites, the local state, and the global system, a negotiation mediated by liberation theology, postcolonial anthropologists and theorists, U.S.-based Latinamericanists, and similarly minded nongovernmental organizations: "Ningun rasgo utópico anima la lucha de la subalternidad étnica en el tercer mundo ni en el primero: se trata de una lucha por insertarse en el sistema establecido" (59) [No trace of utopia animates the struggle of the ethnic subaltern in the third world, or even the first; it is rather a case of wanting to insert itself into the established system]. In this sense, he argues, like Stoll about Menchú's testimonio, that the discourses of Mayan identity politics do not adequately represent, in the double sense of *speaking about* (that is, mimetically), and *speaking for* (that is, politically), the actual life world of indigenous peoples in their multiple accommodations with both the surrounding Ladino, Spanish-speaking world of the nation and global or transnational cultural flows and products. The fact that one of the most prominent exponents of Mayan identity politics in Guatemala, Estuardo Zapeta, openly took a neoliberal position in the debate lends itself to Morales's argument (perhaps too easily, because Zapeta seems an exception in this regard).[9]

Against the sharp (Morales would say Manichean) binaries indigenous/Ladino, dominant/subaltern in both postcolonial theory and Mayan identity politics, Morales advocates instead what he calls a "mestizaje intercultural," which he understands, very much in the manner of Rama's "transculturación narrativa," as a complex and permanent, never completely achieved, process of expression, negotiation, and hybridization of cultural difference. Indeed, in one of the most effective chapters of the book, he argues that *I, Rigoberta Menchú* is as much a hybrid or "mestizo" text as the novels of Miguel Angel Asturias, which tended to be a target of Mayanist critiques.

Morales's concern in attacking the perspectives of postcolonial studies and multiculturalism and their supposed complicity with indigenous identity politics and social movements is nominally with the reconstruction of the Guatemalan Left after the defeat of the armed struggle and in the face of the new challenges posed to the Latin American nation-state by neoliberal economic policies like NAFTA/CAFTA (North American Free Trade Agreement, Central American Free Trade Agreement) and globalization. The specter of a sovereign national space interfered with by foreign interests, including U.S.-style "political correctness" and NGOs, is one of his main concerns. In his view, the rise of indigenous identity politics fragments the potential unity of the nation, which should be based on a commonality that "mestizaje intercultural" both embodies and symbolizes. He concludes:

> La negociación interétnica es un asunto interno de Guatemala, y por ello es deseable y conveniente que lo resolvamos los guatemaltecos sin acudir a tutelajes paternalistas. . . . El país necesita crearse una ideología nacional

lo más integrada posible para enfrentar la globalización con alguna dig-
nidad. Dejemos ya de atrincherarnos detras de identidades esencialistas
como las de indios y ladinos, "mayas" y mestizos, y lleguemos a sentirnos
todos chapines. (419–20)

[Interethnic negotiation is a matter internal to Guatemala, and therefore
it is desirable and convenient that we Guatemalans resolve it without re-
lying on a paternalistic tutelage. . . . The country needs to create the most
integrated national ideology possible in order to confront globalization
with some degree of dignity. Let us then stop entrenching ourselves in essentialist identities like Indians and Ladinos, "Mayas" and mestizos, and
all come to think of ourselves as *chapines*.]

On the face of it, there seems little to object to here, especially since
Morales makes it clear that he does not mean to deploy the idea of mestizaje in the way Vasconcelos or an earlier nationalist and populist Latinamericanism did: "el mestizaje intercultural no evade las especificidades
culturales ni las diferencias" (419) [intercultural mestizaje does not evade
cultural specificities and differences]. But why put the idea of "intercul-
turality" under the rubric of "mestizaje" in the first place then, when mestizaje is itself a form of cultural specificity and difference? It might help
bring into focus what is at issue here to pose the question whether identity
politics is an *obstacle* to the reemergence of the Left, as Morales seems to
feel, or rather a *precondition* for that reemergence? It goes without saying
that *all* culture is, almost by definition, "hybrid" or transcultured, and we
have all come to understand the possible limitations of identity politics
in a global neoliberal framework that has no problem with niche markets
and "difference." However, it seems to me (but then part of the force of
Morales's argument is to try to disqualify my authority to speak in this
regard) that an "interethnic" political bloc articulated from the left that
could bid for hegemony in a country like Guatemala and at the same time
represent an effective articulation of national identity within globalization—a form of "critical regionalism," to recall the term used by Alberto
Moreiras—should not be founded on a *normative* idea of the hybridization of cultural difference or "mestizaje"; rather, it is precisely racial, class,
gender, ethnic, linguistic differences (including the concrete experience
of being mestizo and poor, as opposed to Morales's somewhat idealized
notion that we are all mestizos or chapines, in effect) in a deeply unequal
society in every sense that would empower the Left as a genuinely repre-

sentative and transformative force. Morales seems to feel that mestizaje is necessary as the expression of a "common" ground—something like what Ernesto Laclau calls an "empty signifier"—because the nation-state requires some form of unitary identity to exist as such. But that requirement of a common identity was the problem the formation of postcolonial nation-states in the Americas posed from the start: the requirements of "citizenship" in the nation-state did not and could not coincide with the territorialities of indigenous social formations or the existence of other nationalities within the supposedly homogeneous national space (for example, Spanish-speakers in the United States). To repeat the question I posed at the end of chapter 2, can the nation be a culturally plural or heterotopic space, or must it have a "singular" identity ("We are all mestizos")? In other words, could it be that it is *from* multicultural difference that the possibility of reconstituting, or perhaps of constituting genuinely for the first time, the Latin American Left appears? The question concerns not only the *means* of the Left—its forms of organization and strategy— but also the nature of its ultimate *ends*, that is a society that is at once egalitarian *and* diverse.

Mutatis mutandis, that is also the question that Mabel Moraña's essay on Borges's story "El etnógrafo" raises. The essay expands on and refines certain positions developed in her well-known polemic "El *boom* del subalterno," which appeared in the late 1990s, at a time when the debate about the pertinence of postcolonial perspectives to Latin American studies was beginning to heat up.[10] Moraña has served as a kind of arbiter of the academic field of Latin American literary and cultural criticism. So it is not surprising that what is at stake in her essay is the relation between the field of Latin American literary criticism as such and a subaltern "otherness" that threatens to destabilize it.

To recall briefly Borges's very short short story: A graduate student in anthropology at a Midwestern university in the United States, Fred Murdock, spends two years on an Indian reservation gathering materials for his dissertation. In the course of his fieldwork he passes through the rituals of indoctrination into the tribe and receives from the tribal shaman "su doctrina secreta." He returns to the university, but announces to his thesis advisor that he does not intend to reveal the secret, or finish his thesis, because it is the process that led him to the knowledge rather than the knowledge itself that he finds important. This renunciation effectively ends his academic career. Borges concludes laconically: "Fred se casó, se divorció, y es ahora uno de los bibliotecarios de Yale" [Fred got married, got divorced, and now is a librarian at Yale].

Moraña uses "El etnógrafo" to critique the privileging of otherness in cultural anthropology and cultural theory. The essay gestures toward an acknowledgment of the force of postcolonial and subaltern perspectives in the Latin American field. But what emerges from a close reading of its argument is a discomfort with multiculturalism and identity politics very similar to that expressed by Morales. The precise culprit is not named, but it would not be stretching things too much to see it as the idea of "barbarian theorizing," to use Walter Mignolo's phrase, in postcolonial criticism — that is, pretending to think or speak from the place of the other. And more broadly, perhaps, the project of a specifically Latin American form of postcolonial or subaltern studies, to the extent that, in Moraña's view, such a project risks the fetishization of the Latin American subject as an orientalized, pretheoretical "other."

Here are some characteristic passages from the essay that express this concern:

En el menú teórico que el debate postmodernista ha ofrecido a la voracidad disciplinaria figuran, entre los platos principales, el del descubrimiento del Otro. . . . Nociones como multiculturalismo, subalternidad, hibridación, heterogeneidad, han sido ensayados como parte de proyectos teóricos que intentan abarcar el problema de la *diferencia* cultural como uno de los puntos neurálgicos del latinoamericanismo actual. Sin embargo, pronto se ha hecho evidente que la simple postulación del registro diferencial no hace, en muchos casos, sino invertir el esencialismo que caracteriza el discurso identitario de la modernidad en distintos momentos de su desarrollo. (104)

[On the theoretical menu that the postmodern debate has offered to disciplinary appetites, there figures among the main dishes the discovery of the Other. . . . Notions like multiculturalism, subalternity, hybridization, heterogeneity have been rehearsed as components of theoretical projects that seek to approach the problem of cultural difference as one of the crucial points of contemporary Latinamericanism. However, it has rapidly become clear that the simple postulation of a differential register often does little more than invert the essentialism that characterizes modernity's discourse of identity at different moments.]

¿Es la *otredad* el dispositivo—el subterfugio—a parte del cual el sujeto de la modernidad se reinscribe dentro del horizonte escéptico de la postmodernidad refundando y refuncionalizando su centralidad como constructor/gestor/administrador de la *diferencia*? (106)

[Is *otherness* the device—the subterfuge—from which the subject of modernity reinscribes itself within the skeptical horizon of postmodernity, refounding and reinstituting its centrality as that which constructs/manages/administers *difference*?]

Se ha recurrido al concepto de "posiciones de sujeto" el cual resulta, como Laclau explica, relativamente útil aunque insuficiente para captar el sentido de la Historia como totalidad. Para ser entendida como tal, ésta requiere de la existencia de un sujeto capaz de organizar experiencia y discurso para llegar al "conocimiento absoluto" . . . de procesos totales. En muchas teorizaciones, sin embargo, podría alegarse que la reformulación de la dinámica entre identidad y alteridad se basa justamente en la crisis de la idea de totalidad histórica y su sustitución por el conjunto de microhistorias o historias "menores" abarcables, ellas sí, desde posiciones de sujeto variables y acotadas. (105)

[There has been a resort to the concept of "subject positions" which, as Laclau explains, turns out to be relatively useful although insufficient to capture the sense of History as totality. For History to be understood as such requires the existence of a subject capable of organizing experience and discourse so as to reach an "absolute knowledge" . . . of total processes. In many theorizations, however, one might claim that the reformulation of the dynamic between identity and alterity is based precisely on the crisis of the idea of historical totality and its replacement by an ensemble of microhistories and "minor" histories that can be produced from varied and variously contoured subject positions.]

What is exemplary for Moraña in Borges's story is Murdock's act of renunciation itself. Unlike testimonio or theoretical discourses that claim, in the interests of "solidarity," to let the subaltern speak for itself, or to speak in the name of the subaltern,

el autor de 'El etnógrafo' parece sugerir que la culpa del colonialismo no puede ser expiada de manera definitiva—no, al menos, a través de la cultura, no a partir de lo que Clifford llama "la arena carnavalesca de la diversidad," no por las seducciones de la polifonía ni por las promesas de la heteroglosia, ni por la que Homi Bhabha llama "anondina noción liberal de multiculturalismo." . . . Borges renuncia a articular *para* el otro y *por* el otro una posición de discurso y sobre todo renuncia a teorizar acerca de su condición y su cultura, y aunque le reconoce cualidad enunciativa, afirma con la borradura de la voz la inutilidad—quizá la improcedencia— de toda traducción. . . . Borges nos devuelve a la soledad y a la promesa de la biblioteca. (121, 122)

[the author of "The Ethnographer" seems to suggest that the guilt of colonialism cannot be expiated in a definitive way—at least, not through culture, nor from what Clifford calls "the carnivalesque arena of diversity," nor from the seductions of polyphony, nor from the promises of heteroglossia, nor from what Homi Bhabha calls "the anodyne liberal notion of multiculturalism." . . . Borges renounces articulating *for* or *on behalf of* the other a discursive position and above all he gives up theorizing about his or her condition and culture, and although he acknowledges an enunciative potential in the other, with the erasure of the other's voice he asserts the uselessness—perhaps the inappropriateness–of all forms of translation. . . . Borges returns us to the solitude and the promise of the library.]

Moraña expands on the political implications of this renunciation in a footnote: "Es como Borges rehusara—*avant la lettre*—transformar 'demandas de reconocimiento' que estan llamadas a culminar en políticas identitarias y multiculturales (Taylor, 'The Politics of Recognition') en una 'política de compulsión' (Appiah) que obliga al otro a asumir la identidad que le ha sido socialmente construida y asignada por su condición étnico, sexual, político" (121, n. 33) [It is as if Borges refuses—*avant la lettre*—to transform "demands for recognition" destined to culminate in multicultural and identity politics (Taylor, "The Politics of Recognition") into a "politics of compulsion" (Appiah) that obliges the other to assume the identity that has been socially constructed and assigned to it by its prior ethnic, sexual, and political condition]. But if we are not to have a politically anodyne liberal multiculturalism, or an epistemologically and ethically dubious "anthropological" recuperation of otherness, what is left? Apparently, for Moraña (or for Borges—it is hard to distinguish who is speaking here), the "promise of the library," that is, literature.

Moraña gestures at several points in her essay to Levinas; she writes, for example, of "a subject represented by Borges in the form of the impossibility of knowledge about and the irreducibility of otherness, or better still, by a negativity that can be neither colonized nor apprehended"— "un sujeto representado por Borges bajo la forma de la imposibilidad de conocimiento y la irreductibilidad de la otredad, o sea, por una negatividad no colonizable ni aprehensible" (120). But the appeal to Levinas is itself symptomatic of one aspect of what I am calling the neoconservative turn.[11] That is because it reduces the problem of difference or subalternity, which is both a political and a cultural problem, to an ethical one, a question of exercising choice, as Murdock does. Borges's story deals in a strikingly original way with the agency of the academic intellectual in relation to the subaltern; but what neither the story nor Moraña's essay makes present is precisely the agency *of the subaltern*, which in the case of the tribe Murdock studies might be something like the Mayan identity politics that Morales attacks in *La articulación de las diferencias*.

The critique of the pretension to speak from or "for" a subaltern other is one thing; it may well be, as Moraña argues, echoing Spivak in "Can the Subaltern Speak?," that such a pretension represents simply an inversion of the gesture of Orientalism—to recall one of the passages in Moraña's essay I quoted earlier: "No hace, en muchos casos, sino invertir el esencialismo que caracteriza el discurso identitario de la modernidad."[12] But what is clear is that the decision to leave the other on the side of silence, "en la otra orilla," as Moraña puts it (122), is also a kind of Orientalism, which speaks in the name of the authority of literature to disqualify the effort of indigenous and subaltern subjects to write *themselves* into history. Because what is asked for in identity politics is not so much the *recognition* of difference as the inscription of that difference into the identity of the nation and its history. So the same problem arises as in Morales's appeal to "mestizaje intercultural": the possibility of the formation of a new historical bloc at national, continental, and intercontinental levels in Latin America based on alliance politics between social groups (including but not limited to economic classes) with different sorts of experiences, interests, values, worldviews, histories, cultural practices, sometimes even languages, is disavowed in favor of a skeptical lucidity represented by the institution of literature and literary criticism that does not succumb to the illusions of an "anthropological" or testimonial appeal to the authority of subaltern voice or experience.

It is the siren-like nature of that appeal and its potentially negative or ambiguous political consequences that are the objects of Beatriz Sarlo's critique of testimonial and witness narratives—in particular, the voice/ experience of the victims of political repression in Argentina during the so-called Proceso, the period of military dictatorship and savage repression of the Left from the mid-1970s to the mid-1980s—in her *Tiempo pasado: Cultura de la memoria y giro subjetivo*. Sarlo's argument has its roots in an earlier, much anthologized essay by her on cultural studies and the problem of value.[13] There, very much in the spirit of the critique of the "culture industry" by Adorno and the Frankfurt school, Sarlo was concerned with the way in which standards of literary and aesthetic value were blurred or lost in the appeal to mass or popular culture made by cultural studies, an appeal she characterized as "media neopopulism." In *Tiempo pasado*, by contrast, her concern is with the way in which the vogue for testimonio weakens the possibility of a deeper literary, historical, and sociological reflection on the Proceso. But, as we will see, for Sarlo that concern also involves her marking a distance with a contemporary form of "populism" represented by the neo-Peronism of the Kirchner governments.

The political and ethical authority conceded to testimonio threatens, in Sarlo's view, to destabilize the authority of both imaginative literature and the academic social sciences. This is so because it privileges a simulacrum of subaltern "experience" and voice: that is what Sarlo means by the "giro subjetivo" of the title. Although that privileging is done, usually, in the interests of solidarity and human rights initiatives—for example, Nunca Más or the Madres de la Plaza de Mayo—Sarlo feels that it is paradoxically complicit with the market, and in particular with the fashion for confessional or autobiographical narratives (often of film stars or sports figures) in the media. It is almost as if testimonio, instead of being the record of the victims of neoliberalism and at the same time a form of agency directed against it, were itself a product of neoliberalism, a kind of reality show of human suffering.

Though Sarlo does not take up the wide-ranging discussion or debate over testimonio in the U.S. academy in the 1990s, *Tiempo pasado* might be seen in some ways as a more philosophical version of a book I have already had occasion to mention here: David Stoll's *Rigoberta Menchú and the Story of All Poor Guatemalans*. Like Stoll, Sarlo is concerned both with how testimonio erodes standards of disciplinary authority and boundaries, and how it engenders new forms of "subjective" politics: solidarity politics, founded on empathy, and identity politics, founded on the personal perception of loss or injustice in one's own racial, ethnic, class, or gender identity. In his argument against the authority of Menchú's testimonio, Stoll claimed, for example, that "it was in the name of multiculturalism that Rigoberta Menchú entered the university reading lists" (243); "Under the influence of postmodernism (which has undermined confidence in a single set of facts), and identity politics (which demands acceptance of claims of victimhood), scholars are increasingly hesitant to challenge certain kinds of rhetoric" (244); "The identity needs of Rigoberta's academic constituency play into the weakness of the rules of evidence in postmodern scholarship" (247).

Sarlo similarly attacks what she sees as the pseudo-immediacy and authenticity of testimonial voice, contrasting it to what she calls "la buena historia académica" (16). The authority of academic or professional history has been eroded by the forces of the market and the mass media: "Como la dimensión simbólica de las sociedades en que vivimos esta organizada por el mercado, los criterios son el éxito y la puesta en linea con el sentido común de los consumidores. En esa competencia, la historia académica pierde por razones de método, pero también por sus propias restricciones formales e institucionales" (17) [Given that the symbolic dimension of the societies we live in is organized by the market, the criteria are success and being in tune with the common sense of consumers. In this competition, academic history loses for methodological reasons, but also because of its own formal and institutional restrictions]. In the place of critical or disciplinary thought, we now have a post- (or anti-) Kantian "razón del sujeto," or subjective reason. The "giro subjetivo" is in turn connected to the prestige of identity as a category and identity politics as a form of political agency: "A los combates por la historia también se los llama ahora combates por la identidad" (27) [Struggles about history are now also called struggles about identity], Sarlo observes scornfully.

The effect of the giro subjetivo is to establish a "hegemonía moral" that must be problematized, Sarlo believes, in the name of a more clear-headed sense of both critique and politics. "Del lado de la memoria," she writes, echoing Stoll without realizing it, "me parece descubrir la ausencia de la posibilidad de discusión y de confrontación crítica, rasgos que definirían la tendencia a imponer una visión del pasado" (57) [On the side of memory, I sense the absence of the possibility of critical discussion and confrontation, something that would define the tendency to impose a vision of the past]. "Una utopía revolucionaria cargada de ideas [Sarlo

is referring to the revolutionary activism of the early 1970s in Argentina]
recibe un trato injusto si se la presenta solo como fundamentalmente un
drama posmoderno de los afectos" (91) [A revolutionary utopia charged
with ideas is unjustly represented if it is presented as basically a postmodern drama of affects]. A particular concern is that the predominance of
testimonial discourse in the representation of the Proceso does not allow
one to move beyond the doctrine of the "two devils"—that is, the idea
that both the revolutionary Left and the military were responsible for the
crimes that occurred, since there can be equally compelling narratives of
victimization from both sides.

Against testimonio and its "versión ingenua y 'realista' de la experiencia" (162), Sarlo privileges instead three accounts by victims of the Proceso. One is Alicia Partnoy's quietly vivid collection of short stories or
vignettes based on her own experience as a political prisoner, *The Little
School*. The other two are from the social sciences: Pilar Calveiro's *Poder
y desaparición: Los campos de concentración en Argentina*, and Emilio de
Ipola's essay "La bemba." Sarlo praises Partnoy for her transformation of
her own personal experience (Partnoy was imprisoned and tortured in
the school she describes in her book) into a work of literature that speaks
to the general, shared nature of the situation of disappearance and torture,
rather than to her own experience: "No casualmente, *The Little School* em-
pieza con el relato de la captura de Partnoy contado en tercera persona, de
modo que la identificación esta mediada por un principio de distancia"
(71) [Not accidentally, *The Little School* begins with the story of Partnoy's
capture told in the third person, so that the identification [of character
and narrator] is mediated by a principle of distance]. Both Calveiro and
de Ipola are social scientists who, like Partnoy, were tortured and imprisoned during the Proceso. Like Partnoy too, in writing about that experience, "no privilegian la primera persona del relato. . . . [L]a experiencia es
sometida a un control epistemológico que, por supuesto, no surge de ella
sino de las reglas del arte que practican la historia y las ciencias sociales"
(96). "Ambos escriben con un saber disciplinario, tratando de atenerse a
las condiciones metodológicas de ese saber" (97). "Con el borramiento de
la primera persona, la obra de Calveiro no busca legitimidad ni persua-
sión en razones biográficas, sino intelectuales" (115) [They don't privilege
the first-person narrative voice. . . . [T]he experience is submitted to an
epistemological control that, of course, does not emerge from [the experi-

ence itself] but from the rule of art that history and the social sciences practice. . . . Both write with a disciplinary knowledge, attempting to stay within the methodological conditions of that knowledge. . . . With the erasure of the first-person voice, Calveiro's work does not look for legitimacy or persuasiveness in biographical reasons but rather intellectual ones].

The strong binary opposition between intellectual and biographical reasons—"razones biográficas"/"intelectuales"—in this last statement is notable. It betrays a similar tendency throughout the book. Sarlo has to admit that in the case of Calveiro, "probablemente el libro no hubiera sido escrito si no hubieran existido razones biográficas" (115) [the book would probably not have been written if it were not for biographical reasons]. So why is she so insistent on saying that there cannot be an "intellectual" (or even an aesthetic) dimension to a testimonial or autobiographical narrative, or, vice versa, that "razones intelectuales" cannot have a biographical or experiential dimension? How would she propose to distinguish between, say, Augustine's Confessions and Me llamo Rigoberta Menchú, or Hegel and Kierkegaard?[14]

Though Sarlo does not make the point in so many words in Tiempo pasado, the tendency to impose through a logic of identification or empathy a vision of the past—"imponer una visión del pasado"—is also a specifically political problem that separates what she considers a legitimate left position from a supposedly leftist neopopulism that she rejects.[15] She had spoken in an earlier essay of an "izquierda testimonial, que se refugie en la reafirmación moral-formal de sus valores" [a testimonial Left that seeks refuge in the moral-formal reaffirmation of its values], opposing to it a "political" Left that would be in alliance with an "antimimetic" (i.e., essentially modernist) "cultural" Left: "Ser de izquierda hoy es intervenir en el espacio público y en la política refutando los pactos de mimesis que son pactos de complicidad o de resignación" [To be on the Left today is to intervene in the public sphere and in politics by refuting the mimetic pacts that are pacts of complicity or resignation].[16] The giro subjetivo of testimonio with its emphasis on affect over critical theory, empathy over analysis, is in that sense the corollary of something like Kirchner's neo-Peronism for her. A bad cultural practice—the giro subjetivo—leads to bad politics (because for Sarlo, Kirchner, and now his wife too are bad politics). It is best to leave both in the hands of "experts."[17]

I don't mean to homogenize the political or critical stances of these three authors. They would be the first to indicate points of divergence among themselves. But I think it is possible to see several shared themes running through their arguments, as I have presented them here.

First, a rejection of the authority of subaltern voice and experience, and an extreme dissatisfaction with or skepticism about multiculturalism (or to use the term preferred in Latin American discussions, *interculturalidad*) and identity politics. In particular, the notion of a multicultural historical bloc, similar to that represented in the United States by the idea of the Rainbow Coalition, is rejected or problematized.

Second, a defense of the writer-critic, and (in the fashion of Hannah Arendt) of his/her republican-civic responsibility and authority. Related to this defense is a sense in all three writers of belonging to a generation of the Left that put itself at considerable risk during a difficult period in each of their respective countries, but that is now middle-aged and in the process of being displaced by new political forces and actors. Rather than seeking identification with these new actors, who more often than not do not come from the intelligentsia and either do not share or openly question its values, Sarlo and Morales in particular see them, somewhat ungenerously, as illegitimate or naive.[18]

Third, a reaffirmation in all three writers (and in spite of their explicit or implicit rejection of "identity politics") of a Latin American *criollo* subjectivity in opposition to what is seen as the Anglo-American character of postmodernist or postcolonial theory. This emphasis, in which there is, of course, also an "essentialism" (acknowledged by Morales, but not by Moraña or Sarlo), makes the neoconservative turn a variation in some ways of neo-Arielism: that is, the assumption that the cultural identity and values of Latin America are bound up in some especially significant way with its written literature.

Fourth, a notable failure in all three to come to terms with what Anibal Quijano has called "the coloniality of power" in Latin America—that is, the persistence of cultural/economic/political institutions and racial and gender hierarchies based on colonial forms of rule, long after colonial rule as such in the formal sense has passed from the scene.[19] (Moraña and Morales register the problem of *colonialism*, but see it as one that has been, or can be overcome in the "national" period of their respective countries.) This leads in turn to a failure—particularly striking in the case of Morales, who comes from a country where over half the population is indigenous—to recognize the forms of autonomous political and cultural agency developed by social movements like the indigenous movements in the Andes or Guatemala, or the women's movement.

Fifth, an explicit disavowal of the project of the armed revolutionary struggle of the 1960s and 1970s, in favor of a more considered and cautious Left, with the suggestion that a similar "error" is at the heart of the new politics of identity and empathy. This involves an implicit biographical narrative of personal disillusion or *desengaño* (all three writers are in late middle age, and were active on the Left at one time).[20]

Finally, in all three but especially in Sarlo, a reterritorialization of the academic disciplines and their methodologies and rules against the disruptions of what Néstor García Canclini called "nomad sciences." In the case of literature and literary studies in particular, this entails an affirmation of the canon and canonicity (aesthetic "value" for Sarlo; "la promesa de la biblioteca" for Moraña), not so much as a repository of an a priori cultural authority—Sarlo is, after all, a modernist—but as something that has the depth and consistency to be usefully scrutinized by new generations.

This last is a crucial point, because the neoconservative turn in Latin American criticism, like the U.S. neoconservatives in the so-called culture wars, makes literature and considerations of literary and aesthetic value a central concern, rather than something that is supplementary or secondary. Sarlo is especially eloquent in this regard at the end of her book: "La literatura, por supuesto, no disuelve todos los problemas planteados, ni puede explicarlos, pero en ella un narrador siempre piensa *desde fuera* de la experiencia, como si los humanos pudieran apoderarse de la pesadilla y no sólo padecerla" (166) [Literature, of course, does not dissolve all the problems posed, nor can it explain them, but within it a narrator always thinks *from outside* experience, as though human beings could take control of the nightmare rather than simply endure it]. But all three texts, not just Sarlo's, are "defenses of literature," aimed at policing the frontiers of what is permissible and what is not within the field of Latin American literary and cultural criticism, at a moment in which many of its foundational assumptions, including the idea of Latin America itself,[21] have come under question from within and without.

One can argue of course that I am overstating the case and that the kind of critical operation represented by these three texts is something quite different from neoconservatism of the sort espoused by figures such as Samuel Huntington, Allan Bloom, or Dinesh D'Souza in the U.S. culture wars, for example, or someone like Octavio Paz in his later years in Latin America. All three writers still consider themselves persons of the Left, and think of their positions as precisely a *defense* of the Left—a Left rooted in the ideas of human progress, emancipation, the nation, reason, science, and secularism that is not afraid to ask radical, structural questions about the nature of the state and society, against postmodernist relativism and the "weak" multiculturalism of identity politics. But, while my own position is not an entirely disinterested one (many of the critical points made by Morales, Moraña, and Sarlo pertain directly or indirectly to aspects of my own work), I don't think I am overstating the case. I am trying to capture a tendency that is emerging, but that has not become fully conscious of itself as such yet, and may move in several different ways (nor do I mean to necessarily conflate the positions of Morales, Moraña, and Sarlo, which have significant points of difference). My prediction is that what I am calling the neoconservative turn will remain a tendency *within* the Latin American Left, bidding to influence its goals and limits. That is, it will be, like Daniel Bell's position alluded to earlier, "conservative" in cultural matters but "liberal" in political and economic ones. But it is also possible that, as the political situation in Latin America itself becomes more polarized, the neoconservative turn may move to align itself politically with an explicitly conservative or center-right position, as happened with the New York Intellectuals in the United States or with the so-called New Philosophers or the historian François Furet in the wake of May 1968 in France. The examples of Jorge Castañeda in Mexico and Elisabeth Burgos in Venezuela are suggestive of this possible outcome, I think.

As I argued earlier apropos neo-Arielism, the denial of the possibility of transnational solidarity is above all a denial of the ability of the gringo or non–Latin American to understand and "represent" Latin America. In a situation where both Latin America's past and future involve a confrontation with the power of the United States at all levels, that is fair enough. But there is also in the neoconservative position a denial of the possibility of solidarity between groups of different ethnic, cultural, social, and linguistic formation *within* the confines of a given Latin American nation-state or across national borders in Latin America as a region.

Yet solidarity politics and human rights mobilizations have been among the most effective forms that social movements in Latin America have developed both locally and globally against the force of globalization and repressive or anachronistic states. And the idea of a political movement or "front" based on "alliance politics" rather than a specific party is essential in many of the new governments of the marea rosada, including especially (but not only) Bolivia and Ecuador. While I do not intend by any means to foreclose debate and discussion within the Left, or about the Left in Latin America, it seems to me that there is implicit in the neoconservative turn something like the doctrine of the "two Lefts" I spoke about in the introduction: in other words, the Brazilian PT and perhaps Tabaré in Uruguay and Funes in El Salvador (the "respectable Left") versus every one else, especially Chávez and Morales, but also López Obrador, the Kirchners (husband and wife), Correa, the Sandinistas, Ollantá, Lugo, the Cubans . . . (the "retrograde Left"). In Brazil, the "respectable Left" is in power, and in Chile it was until recently. But in Argentina, Bolivia, or Venezuela, it sometimes forms part of the opposition to the new governments of the Left in power. That sector of the "old" Left that has become part of the opposition to the governments of the marea rosada is often coincident with what I mean by the neoconservative turn. To return to a point I made earlier, this development recalls strongly the critique of the New Left in the United States, especially of the emerging identity politics of feminism and radical black nationalism, advanced in the early 1970s by some of the figures who were to become in later life neoconservatives. My concern is that in a similar fashion what I am calling the neoconservative turn in Latin America has the potential to divide unnecessarily the new Latin American Left and inhibit its emerging hegemonic force at both the national and the continental levels. But I suppose too that the question is where the line between necessary and unnecessary differences is drawn, where one passes from "critical support" or legimate criticism into outright opposition.[22]

What are the social roots of the impulse behind the neoconservative turn? I lack the disciplinary competence to answer this question adequately. But I will venture the hypothesis that it is a superstructural effect of two developments related to the impact of globalization on Latin America during the period of the Washington consensus: (1) the crisis of certain sectors of the Latin American middle and upper middle class, including the intelligentsia, affected in contradictory ways by neoliberal structural adjustment policies, the weakening of state support for higher education and for education generally, and the spread of commercialized mass culture; and (2) the recent weakening of the ideological hegemony of neoliberalism itself.

Neoliberal ideology is increasingly seen in Latin America and else-where as insufficient in itself to guarantee governability. In Latin America in particular, especially in the late 1990s and the early years of the new century, the consequences of neoliberal economic policies produced a legitimation crisis of both the state and the ideological apparatuses, in-cluding the school, the family, religious institutions, and the traditional system of political parties. The inherent libertarianism implicit in the "rational choice" model of decision making proved unable to serve as a basis for imposing on populations a normative structure of values and expectations. At the same time, the combination of privatization and the spread of commercialized global mass culture destabilized the cultural authority of a previous system of norms, standards, and hierarchies, and threatened the economic well-being of sectors of the upper and profes-sional middle classes that intellectuals, whatever their stated ideologies, tend to come from and represent.

We have all come to understand that global capitalism still *requires* the nation-state in some ways: to keep populations in line, to ensure gov-ernability, to protect investments and private property, and to instill a self-disciplined character structure capable of postponing immediate gratification in the expectation of eventual reward. (The nation-state has become something like the proverbial "neighborhood policeman" in globalization.)[23] The neoconservative turn offers itself as, in effect, a new ideology of professionalism and disciplinarity, centered on the sphere of the humanities, which were particularly devalued and damaged by neo-liberal reforms in education, an ideology implemented by and through the state and the state ideological apparatuses to counter the legitimation crisis provoked by neoliberalism.

If this hypothesis is correct, and I emphasize its tentative character, then the neoconservative turn in Latin American criticism could be seen as an attempt by a middle- and upper-middle-class, university-educated, and essentially white, criollo-Ladino intelligentsia to recapture the space of cultural and hermeneutic authority from two forces that are also them-selves in contention with each other: the first being the hegemony of neo-liberalism and what are seen as the negative consequences of the un-controlled or unmediated force of the market and commercialized mass culture; and the second, social movements and political formations based in identity politics or "populisms" of various sorts, which involve new political and cultural actors no longer necessarily beholden to the political or strategic leadership of a university-educated, and ethnically mainly European or criollo-mestizo intelligentsia.

The disciplinary modesty of the critique offered in these three cases, which limit themselves to the academic sphere of literary and cultural criticism, should not conceal their wider ambitions and implications. More or less explicitly, and with notable intellectual rigor and eloquence, they at once make an appeal to the intelligentsia and professional classes for a new form of cultural hegemony, understood in Gramsci's sense of "the moral and intellectual leadership of the nation," which incorporates their own disciplinary standards of professionalism and specialization, and attempt to redefine (and confine) the newly emergent project of the Latin American Left, nourished from below by very heterogeneous popular-subaltern social actors, within parameters that continue to be dominated by the intelligentsia and the professional classes.

Both Moraña and Sarlo invoke a return to Borges, and Morales offers a rehabilitation of Asturias, which amounts for our present purposes to the same thing. This rehabilitation of Borges marks a point of convergence between the neoconservative turn and deconstruction. Borges, of course, has never entirely disappeared from the horizon of Latin American literary and cultural criticism. The reasons for this are not hard to discern: he remains in his disillusioned lucidity and his capacity for literary invention perhaps the most fascinating Latin American literary intellectual of the twentieth century. Moreover, that disillusioned lucidity seemed to fit well with the aftermath of the defeat of the revolutionary Left and the end of an era of utopian illusions. Borges's own penchant for inhabiting the boundary between self and other, representation and reality, territory and map makes his own writing a kind of Aleph that allows us to read into it, as Moraña does in the essay discussed here, the burning issues of the day: the other, deconstruction, ethics, testimonio, the subaltern, cultural and postcolonial studies, the dialectics of a peripheral modernity, the Benjaminian "illumination" in a Latin American key. But to read those issues into Borges, or with Borges, is also in a way to limit those issues *to* Borges—that is, to the space of imaginative literature.

In this way, the appeal to Borges runs the risk of becoming the figure for the neoconservative turn as such, in much the same way that T. S. Eliot was in Anglo-American criticism of the period of the Cold War. The threat of an *actual* subaltern "other"—that potentially lethal and usually racialized presence at the edges of Borges's stories, which is finally (as in

"El Sur") a threat to decenter the political and epistemological authority of the "lettered city" as such — is neutralized or postponed, and we return to the private and disillusioned, but finally *adequate* consolations of literature and literary criticism: "la promesa de la biblioteca."

It is not that the appeal to Borges is in itself reactionary. What is problematic rather is the failure in making that appeal to register adequately the connection between Borges's epistemological and aesthetic strategies and his reactionary and often racist political positions.[24]

I close with the question of Borges, because I think it is a particularly difficult one for us. As in the case of Shakespeare or Cervantes, Borges *is* literature, and literature is, finally, what those of us who work in the field of literary and cultural criticism do as intellectuals. To what extent then are we also, individually and collectively, invested in what I am calling the neoconservative turn? This is a variant of the question that is at the heart of the Christian Gospels: whom do you serve? The particular difficulty of the times we live in and of our institutional location and loyalties is that it is easier to ask this question than to answer it.

Beyond the Paradigm of Disillusion:
Rethinking the Armed Struggle in Latin America

How is the armed struggle in Latin America remembered today, a generation after its historical defeat or collapse? That is a different question from
whether one advocated armed struggle in the past (or would advocate it
in the present). Bill Clinton famously remarked that how one views the
sixties remains the basic fault line in U.S. culture, providing among other
things the best measure of whether one votes Republican or Democrat. I
want to suggest here that there is a relation between how one thinks about
the armed struggle in Latin America and how one thinks about the nature
and possibilities of the new governments of the marea rosada, even where
these have explicitly moved away from the model of armed struggle.

The most cynical verdict on the sixties I am aware of is a remark attributed to Regis Debray: "We thought we were heading to China, but we
ended up in California." But at least the juxtaposition preserves something of the—admittedly often wildly incongruous—utopian impulses
behind that era. Much more melancholic is Beatriz Sarlo's comment in
an op-ed piece in a major Buenos Aires newspaper some years ago apropos the armed struggle in her own country: "Muchos sabemos por experiencia que se necesitaron años para romper con estas convicciones. No
simplemente para dejarlas atrás porque fueron derrotadas, sino porque
significaron una equivocación" [Many of us know from experience that it
took years to break with these beliefs [in armed struggle]. Not simply to
leave them behind or because they were defeated, but because they were
a mistake].[1]

Sarlo's comment came in the context of her critique of the government of Kirchner and what she saw as his demagogic neo-Peronist populism, whose roots, she suggested, are in the same illusions that fed the armed struggle (a criticism she has also extended to Kirchner's wife and successor, Cristina Fernández). Sarlo speaks from having held herself a position close to the armed struggle in Argentina at one time, so there is a sense of personal miscalculation and remorse behind her stance. Similarly, the Venezuelan writer Elisabeth Burgos, Debray's wife during the period of his collaboration with Che Guevara (and who subsequently worked with Rigoberta Menchú in the creation of her famous testimonial narrative), has in recent years combined a posture of disillusion with the armed struggle with an active involvement in the opposition to Chávez in Venezuela, a position she shares with one of the most famous Venezuelan guerrilla leaders, Teodoro Petkoff (and Debray himself long ago broke off his connection with the Cubans and regards his enthusiasm for the armed struggle today as a youthful, ultraleftist folly). These examples could easily be multiplied. They configure what I will call a *paradigm of disillusion* in the representation of the armed struggle in Latin America.

By "the armed struggle" I mean the historical period or cycle in Latin America that, very broadly speaking, extends, with regional variations, from the 1960s through the end of the 1980s. It is inaugurated in Latin America as a whole by the victory of the Cuban revolution in 1959. In South America, with the exception of Peru and Colombia, it extends to the overthrow of Allende in 1973 and the subsequent imposition of rightwing military dictatorships in Chile, Argentina, and Uruguay. In Central America, which has a different regional dynamic, the armed struggle gestates in the sixties, stalls in the early seventies, achieves the triumph of the Nicaraguan revolution in 1979 and strong insurgencies in El Salvador and Guatemala, is then challenged by the counterinsurgency campaigns of the early and mid-1980s and the Contra war, and ends with the Sandinistas' electoral defeat in February 1990 (and the subsequent peace negotiations between the guerrillas and the government in El Salvador and Guatemala).

The armed struggle in Latin America had many different forms. But the basic idea behind it might be expressed as follows (I derive this inevitably from Che Guevara's manual *Guerrilla Warfare* and Regis Debray's gloss of this in *Revolution in the Revolution*). The objective possibility for political change was latent in the conditions of poverty, inequality, racial discrimination, underdevelopment, and authoritarian or dictatorial rule present in Latin American countries for centuries. What was lacking were the subjective conditions, the confidence that if people were to rise up, they could actually win. The masses were trapped in a condition of passivity and resignation imposed by military force and racial and class violence. Socialist and communist parties were limited to seconding the reformist demands of the modernizing sectors of the national bourgeoisie, focusing their demands on the restoration of democracy, economic development, trade union rights, human rights. In order to detonate the revolutionary potential latent in Latin American societies, some sort of spark was needed. The armed struggle was that spark. In Guevara's famous metaphor, the guerrilla vanguard or *foco* would be the "small motor" that started the "large motor" of society as a whole. Simply by being able to engage with the army and police and survive, the foco—sometimes, as in the case of the Cuban insurrection, no more than several dozen actual armed combatants initially (albeit with an extensive support network)—would demonstrate to the rest of society that it was possible to challenge the status quo. As people absorbed that idea, the movement would pass from the stage of small-scale guerrilla actions against very limited targets to the stage of a general insurrection, involving widespread social and political mobilization and unrest. It was that general insurrection, rather than the ability to defeat the army and police in direct military combat, that would provide the conditions for victory of the armed struggle.

There were some immediate and powerful objections. First, of course, was the ethical injunction against violence, and in particular the commandment "Thou shall not kill." To choose the path of armed struggle, even where it was posed as a means of liberating millions of people from centuries of poverty and oppression, meant that one had to accept the possibility of killing (and being killed), destroying property, and polarizing society into bitterly antagonistic camps of friends and enemies.[2] There was also a more pragmatic objection, especially from those sectors of the Latin American Left, including the leadership of most of the important communist and socialist parties, who thought the best path for social progress was through incremental reforms. They argued, not without some reason, that the strategy of armed struggle was unwise politically, because it risked alienating sectors of the population that otherwise might be sympathetic to the Left, and invited the repressive apparatus of the state to come down directly against the Left and its political allies.

Part of the problem of remembering the armed struggle is that while there are adequate histories of the armed struggle in this or that country, there is no history—at least none that I am aware of—that deals with the armed struggle as a general historical phenomenon in Latin America. Debray himself began such a history in a project called *Crítica de las armas* (*The Critique of Arms*) back in the 1970s, but abandoned it as his own political career shifted rightward (there are, nevertheless, remnants of that critique in the recent volumes of his autobiography). Up to now the most comprehensive and influential attempt in Latin America itself to sum up the experience of the armed struggle is probably Jorge Castañeda's book, *Utopia Unarmed* (published 1994), which featured interviews with and portraits of some of the major guerrilla leaders.[3] But *Utopia Unarmed* turned out to be a somewhat premature obituary for the armed struggle (the Zapatista uprising in Chiapas broke out just before its publication), and it would serve more as a launching pad for the author's opportunistic ambitions as a neoconservative politician in Mexico than as an anticipation of the new forms of left politics that were gestating in Latin America in the 1990s. David Stoll's attack on Rigoberta Menchú in his 1999 book, *Rigoberta Menchú and the Story of All Poor Guatemalans*, with its charge that Menchú had misrepresented aspects of her story in order to shore up support for the guerrillas, was also, perhaps even mainly, an attack on the armed struggle in Guatemala. Stoll argues in particular that rural guerrilla strategies "are an urban romance, a myth propounded by middle-class radicals who dream of finding true solidarity in the countryside," a myth that has "repeatedly been fatal for the left itself, by dismaying lower-class constituencies and guaranteeing a crushing response from the state."[4]

My underlying assumption is that, while there are many good reasons to be critical of or skeptical about the armed struggle, a vision of it as an "equivocación," or error, as in Sarlo, even when it is produced from what is nominally a leftist position, sustains neoliberal hegemony in Latin America, in the same way that an antisixties narrative underlies the neoconservative turn in the United States. That hegemony is on the wane, and the Latin American Left has made significant gains; many of the people involved in the governments of the marea rosada, or in the movements that brought them to power, cut their political teeth in the period of the armed struggle (these include Dilma Roussef, the candidate of the Partido dos Trabalhadores [PT] and winner in the recent (2010) presidential elections in Brazil). The new forms of thought and practice that correspond to this tectonic shift in Latin American politics—in other words, what I mean in this book by "Latinamericanism after 9/11"—cannot be articulated without reassessing the heritage of the armed struggle. Yet, except for a partial rehabilitation of the figure of Che Guevara in recent years—for example, in Walter Salles's popular film version of Guevara's *The Motorcycle Diaries* or the two-part film biography of Che by Steven Soderbergh—the armed struggle remains largely bracketed away from public memory in Latin America, almost like the strike of the plantation workers in Gabriel García Márquez's *One Hundred Years of Solitude*. This is so partly because young people in Latin America today, unlike Sarlo's or my generation, have in general no direct biographical connection to the armed struggle. But that inevitable generation gap is aggravated in turn by the fact that the representations of the armed struggle they do have access to, like Castañeda's *Utopia Unarmed*, give on the whole a negative image of it. That image is in turn governed by what I am calling here the paradigm of disillusion.

The paradigm of disillusion rests on a coming-of-age narrative that describes the Latin American generation that sixties figures such as Sarlo, Burgos, or Castañeda belonged to—a generation, or a significant part of it, that defined itself as being committed to or in solidarity with the armed struggle. Its underlying idea is something like the following: The illusion of the revolutionary transformation of society that was the inspiration for armed struggle was a kind of romantic adolescence. It was a generous and brave adolescence, but also one prone to excess, error, irresponsibility, and moral anarchy. By contrast, the biological and biographical maturity of the generation of the sixties represented by our role and responsibilities as parents and professionals corresponds to the hegemony of neoliberalism and political redemocratization in the 1980s and 1990s.

The portrait of the hit man, El Chivo, in the third part of the Mexican film *Amores perros* can serve as an example of the paradigm of disillusion for our purposes here. The character is depicted as a former university professor, who, idealistically, abandoned his wife and child to become a guerrilla in the wake of the 1968 massacres in Mexico City, then got involved in a kidnapping for ransom, and was captured and imprisoned for twenty years as a consequence. Now—in the chaotic neoliberal present of Mexico City that the film so vividly captures—he is working as a hired killer for the policeman who captured him. He is bearded, shabbily dressed, difficult to distinguish from a street person. It is not clear whether the director intended this, but with his beard, the character looks strikingly like Marx. At the end of the film, after he has renounced serving as a hired killer, he shaves the beard off and makes an at least symbolic reconciliation with the daughter he abandoned as a child (leaving some money and a long phone message for her). He can never return to what he once was; but he is no longer Marx, so to speak.[5] The implication is that his decision to join the guerrillas was both immature and unethical, a kind of "sin" like incest or adultery (the moral centers of the other two stories in the film) that he must now attempt to make amends for.

Amores perros is a particularly striking (and well-known) example, but the paradigm of disillusion that operates in the story of El Chivo is present in one form or another in countless novels, testimonial narratives, histories, memoirs, poems, and films about the armed struggle in Latin America. The paradigm is in turn a variation on the model of the picaresque novel, especially what was the most widely read novel in both Spain and its colonies, Mateo Alemán's *Guzmán de Alfarache* (1605). As he approaches maturity, the *pícaro* repents of his or her wicked life, betrays former comrades to the authorities, makes peace with the state and the law, and sits down to write his or her story, which will be instructive — *ejemplar* — for others. The repentant guerrilla — *el guerrillero arrepentido* — has become something like the reincarnation of the baroque pícaro in contemporary Latin American culture.[6]

However, there is a second, and perhaps more deeply entrenched (because it is not so apparent) narrative paradigm at work in the way the armed struggle is remembered, or dismissed, in Latin America today. This has to do with the common sense, but of course ultimately deeply ideological view of history that identifies forward movement in time with progress.[7] Since neoliberalism and regional economic integration under U.S. auspices come *after* the period of revolutionary upsurge, they appear as in some sense or other *inevitable* — a historical stage that transcends the previous stage, creating new constraints and conditions of possibility, such that even the Left, if it is to reemerge, would have to start from there. There can be no going back, even if one wanted to. What happens in the paradigm of disillusion in the representation of the armed struggle (and of the sixties generally) is that a biographical narrative of personal maturation and "success" is mapped onto this underlying narrative of historical transition between one stage and another.

There is no question that in the last thirty or so years, counterrevolutionary state violence, the weakening of the welfare state by neoliberal policies, and the effects of globalization have changed the terrain of political struggle in Latin America dramatically. And this in turn has affected the nature of the Latin American Left and its short- and long-term goals. Arguably, if globalization represents a new stage of capitalism with its own particular contradictions and dynamics, then it requires a new form of socialism, in the same way that Lenin held that imperialism, as the new stage of capitalism emerging with the dawn of the twentieth century, required a different strategy than the socialism of the Second International, rooted in labor unions and parliamentary social democratic parties. Something like this is, of course, the basic idea behind Michael Hardt's and Antonio Negri's *Empire*. However, in my view the historical paradigm that is more immediately pertinent to Latin America is not the idea that globalization under neoliberal auspices represents a new historical stage. It is rather that of a restoration, on the model of the period that follows the death of Napoleon and waning of the radicalizing impulse of the French and Haitian Revolutions between the Congress of Vienna and the revolutionary upsurges of 1848. How would one propose to distinguish a "restoration" from a "new stage" (of history, and of the history of capitalism in particular)? A restoration represents the blockage of a historical process that has already been set in motion, rather than its transcendence—for example, the blockage of the rise of the Spanish bourgeoisie as a class-for-itself in the sixteenth century. To put this another way, the social and economic contradictions that give rise to the process are not structurally modified or transformed by a restoration; they are simply repressed or deferred, prevented from coming to fruition in a new historical stage. But the contradictions continue to be present and active under the surface of the conservative status quo. It is to be expected, then, that the elements of the process will reemerge, albeit in new and sometimes unexpected forms, as the force of the reactionary coalition that produced the restoration in the first place begins to wane over time. Between Metternich and the Congress of Vienna and 1848 in Europe are thirty-four years—roughly a generation. Similarly roughly thirty years separate the defeat of the Left in South America in the mid-1970s, orchestrated by that modern disciple of Metternich, Henry Kissinger, and its recent resurgence (and twenty-eight years separate the elections of Reagan in 1980 and Obama in 2008).

It would be nice to say that, with the advent of democratization, the long historical sequence of violence in Latin America, of which the armed struggle was certainly one form, is over, that politics is now completely absorbed by civil society and the parliamentary electoral system. Nor, as I have said, is it my intention here in taking up the question of armed struggle to advocate it as a strategy in the present. It is clear that on the whole politics and social activism have moved onto a new terrain in Latin America. However, that terrain is articulated in several important ways by the heritage of the armed struggle. And it is not exactly true to say that armed struggle is completely something of the past in Latin America. It continues unabated in large areas of rural Colombia; it reappeared in southern Mexico with the Zapatista uprising of the early 1990s in Chiapas, in part as a response to the implementation of the NAFTA accords; and it has flared up recently in Guerrero and other states of Mexico; indigenous movements in Brazil, Chile, Peru, Ecuador, and elsewhere have resorted to violent protests in their efforts to prevent encroachment by state and private projects on their communal lands.[8] The disappearance of violence at the hands of those outside the state apparatus in Latin America will depend not so much on the will of the state to impose order, or on an understandable desire for order and stability, as on the ability of the state to produce concretely economic prosperity or fairness, and more egalitarian, tolerant, and inclusive social conditions. But for that to happen will require a different kind of state, and that brings us back to the question of what the armed struggle aimed to accomplish.

In retrospect, it seems that the armed struggle was fated to defeat from the start: that is certainly part of the force of Sarlo's judgment that the very idea of armed struggle was an error. But it did not seem so in the sixties; in fact it was the armed struggle and the apparent historical logic it was connected to—the spread of socialism and "wars of national liberation"—that seemed "irreversible" (to use the language of the time). There is no question that many individual projects of armed struggle were ill-conceived and doomed—the Argentine experience that Sarlo refers to among them, in my opinion. But that does not justify the claim that they were *all* ill-conceived or doomed, that victory was impossible from the start. In fact, the armed struggle did set in motion a very pronounced radical political dynamic throughout the Americas (including the United States). Victory was achieved in at least two countries, Cuba and Nicaragua, and armed struggle movements came close to taking power in several other countries. The FMLN (Frente Farabundo Martí para la Liberación Nacional) could plausibly have won, for example, in El Salvador. And if it had won, things on the ground would have been dramatically different in Central America and the Caribbean, including Grenada, and thus in the Americas generally. The balance of power could have "tipped" in another direction entirely.

Although the dynamics of armed struggle were (and continue to be) often quite local and specific, its eventual defeat was certainly deeply connected to the overall waning of the force of the socialist bloc, with the Soviet Union entering in the 1970s a period of deep economic stagnation (which also overtook Cuba after the economic failure of the 1969 sugar harvest), and with China wrestling with the effects of the Cultural Revolution and moving decisively after 1972 toward détente with the United States. Pertinent here too is the prospect that even if the armed struggle had succeeded in other countries of Latin America, at best it would have produced something like Cuba, Vietnam, Algeria, or some of the sub-Saharan African countries "liberated" by armed struggle in the sixties, with all their well-documented problems today. The guerrillero arrepentido might be tempted to say: maybe it was better that we *did not* win.

But that melancholy sense of a historical "inevitability" ultimately confirmed by the collapse of the Soviet Union concedes something it does not have to: that the armed struggle in Latin America depended on the fate of Soviet communism. It might be equally true to say the opposite, in fact: that is, that the fate of the Soviet Union depended on the possibility of Latin America becoming socialist. The paradigm of disillusion is thus a form of historicism, a "personal Thermidor," to recall Alain Badiou's phrase (see note 6), rather than an objective appraisal of historical necessity. For one of the things that was most original and attractive about the armed struggle in Latin America was precisely that it portended a *new* form of socialism that would have differed from the Russian and Chinese models—already perceived at the time as deeply problematic (Che Guevara spoke derisively of "goulash communism")—on the one hand, and West European social democracy, still deeply tied to colonialism and imperialism, on the other. In the Cuban revolution in its glory days, before it became heavily dependent on the Soviet Union, or in Allende's strategy of a democratic "Chilean road to socialism," or in the rural "liberated zones" of this or that region of Colombia or northeastern Brazil, or in the Sandinista experience in Nicaragua, with all its ambiguities and contradictions, what was being gestated were uniquely *Latin American* forms of socialism, in the same way, say, Chinese communism or European social democracy were specific to their respective societies. Those new forms of socialism, had they prospered and begun to sustain and influence one another, would have served in turn as an inspiration and a basis of material support for other processes of liberation. Here one must remember with respect something that is today also largely forgotten (though not by Nelson Mandela): Cuba's crucial role in supporting the eventually successful struggle against the apartheid regime in South Africa, which had an important military dimension (the defeat of the South African army in Angola). But not only in third world or peripheral countries; I note in passing from personal experience the tremendous influence the example of the Latin American revolutionary Left had on the New Left in the United States.

There is no question that the Soviet Union, China, and the European social democrats tried hard to contain the Latin American movements, including the armed struggle as well as other strategies like Allende's, within their respective formulas, but the movements kept breaking out of those formulas with great theoretical and practical originality and daring. Would the collapse of socialism internationally have been "inevitable" if one after another country in Latin America had followed in the path of Cuba in the 1960s? Or if the Guatemalans and Salvadorans had been able to follow in relatively short order the Sandinistas in the early 1980s? If Allende could have made good on his promise of a "Chilean Road to Socialism"? And would Cuba itself have lapsed into authoritarian rigidity and economic stagnation if other Latin American countries had been in a position to have fraternal ties with it?

By invoking Cuba, I mean to raise in particular the question of democracy, which was and is without doubt one of the weak points of the Cuban example. It was part of the Cold War strategy of counterinsurgency (as today in Iraq) to put into opposition formal democracy and armed insurrection. But, in fact, many, perhaps even most of the armed struggle experiences in Latin America (for example, Cuba, Dominican Republic, Guatemala, Nicaragua, Argentina, and Brazil) arose precisely against military dictatorships, or in situations of deep crisis or corruption of political institutions, where legal electoral options were choked off. At the same time, however, it is clear that, with the exception of the Chilean Popular Unity, the Latin American revolutionary Left, based as it was on the notion of a small revolutionary vanguard or elite, did not give enough thought or credence to the question of mass democracy and political hegemony expressed in electoral or cultural terms. And this produces, perhaps, the authoritarian "tendency" noted in the Cuban case or ascribed today to Chávez. Still, I would argue that, on balance, the experience of armed struggle in Latin America, including Cuba, went *in the direction of* democracy, and brought into politics a new spirit of hope for change that had been missing since the 1930s and new possibilities for direct participation. It also raised the prospect of moving beyond the often restrictive and highly manipulated forms of electoral politics and trade unionism to new, more comprehensive and representative, forms of democracy and political participation.

Part of the originality and promise of the armed struggle in Latin America was embodied in its cultural superstructure. For example, while I don't mean to downplay what is happening today in Latin American film, understanding that each new generation has to find its own path of expression, I see nothing that rivals in scope or ambition the great Cuban films of the late sixties and seventies; or the Brazilian *cinema novo*, particularly the work of Glauber Rocha; or the massive documentary reconstruction of the rise and fall of Allende's Popular Unity government, *La batalla de Chile*; or the Argentine masterpiece *La hora de los hornos* (*The Hour of the Furnaces*), one of the most daring and original films produced anywhere in the world in that period, until recently available only in pirated copies, even in Argentina. All of these films and many, many more were deeply related to the impulse of the armed struggle. In similar fashion, the novelists of the Latin American boom, like Gabriel García Márquez or Julio Cortázar, were given to sometimes associating their modernist narrative techniques with the vanguard function of the guerrilla foco.[9] And there was the influential Colombian *teatro de creación colectiva*; a strong strain of "committed" poetry—*poesía militante*—ranging from works by established figures like Ernesto Cardenal, to the politicized pop songs of the Cuban *nueva trova*, and in the Nicaraguan revolution, a *poesía de taller* written by peasants, soldiers, and workers in their own places of work; a politicized and dynamic Pop art; and testimonio—testimonial narrative—whose emergence and authority as a narrative form was deeply connected to the armed struggle. It is not only that many musicians, artists, and writers became fellow travelers of the revolutionary movements, as had been the case in the thirties with figures such as Pablo Neruda or Diego Rivera. The guerrilla movements and their extensive support networks provided a context in which, as happened in the French Resistance during the Second World War, intellectuals, artists, musicians, and middle-class professionals often found themselves working together in close proximity with workers and peasants from the popular sectors (not always unproblematically, but that is another story). I mention in this regard the figure of Roque Dalton in El Salvador, that country's greatest modern writer, who became a guerrilla cadre and was killed in an obscure internecine struggle between factions of his own organization, but only as an indication of a much wider phenomenon.[10]

Like the cultural expressions related to it, the armed struggle was still dominated by what we would call today, after postcolonial theory and cultural studies, a "lettered" creole-mestizo model of Latin American cultural identity. The most politically consequential theoretical articulation of that model was perhaps the idea of "narrative transculturation"—*transculturación narrativa*—advanced by Ángel Rama. In Rama's view, the function of artists, writers, and cultural workers was, in analogy to the catalyzing function of the political vanguard, to bring together the heterogeneous elements of the national reality and to fashion an inclusive cultural identity appropriate to the process of national and regional liberation. That conception, also anticipated in Roberto Fernández Retamar's famous essay "Caliban," was both empowering and limiting, as the sometimes problematic relation of the revolutionary vanguards to indigenous populations or to women and gays revealed. One striking instance of this is the heart-sinking moment in Che's *Bolivian Diary*, when he registers as a kind of unwitting foreshadowing of his own death the unwelcoming, impenetrable stare of the Aymara-speaking peasants he is supposed to be fighting for.

All the armed struggle movements articulated themselves as movements of national liberation. Debray noted back in the 1960s that the key feature of the Latin American armed struggle was its roots in radical nationalism: "Fidel read Martí before reading Lenin."[11] At the same time, however, there was a deep questioning of the adequacy of a traditional sense of the Latin American nation as a vehicle for popular insurgency. The tension between affirmation and critique of the nation-state—a critique that after the waning of the armed struggle was to characterize postmodernist theory—was already present in the debates within the armed struggle itself between national, regional, and continental strategies. Something similar happened with the "identity politics" of the new social movements. As Margaret Randall pointed out apropos the contradictions between the Sandinistas and the women's movement in Nicaragua, it was often only *within* the context of the revolutionary movements that issues of ethnic or women's liberation could begin to be posed as demands in the first place.[12] Moreover, concrete political practice often provided norms for theory, rather than the reverse. Women, gays, regional interests, the vast semiemployed and thus "lumpen" populations of the urban slums, indigenous or Afro-Latin groups began to acquire new identities and agency in the context of their participation in the guerrilla movements or their support networks. In Guatemala, for example, the theoretical premises of an orthodox Marxism, which held that the solution of what was called the "Indian question" was industrialization and proletarianization, were challenged from the armed struggle as more and more indigenous groups actually became involved with it. Che Guevara may have been overly idealistic in his notion of the "New Man," but he was not completely wrong in seeing the human relations created among the members of the guerrilla group as a model for a more liberated, pluralistic, multicultural, and egalitarian Latin American identity. The problem, which Guevara himself was not able to solve, was in translating that model to the population as a whole.

I don't mean to downplay the persistence of voluntarism, authoritarianism, sublimated machismo, and even racism within the revolutionary Left—my own involvement with the project of subaltern studies was in part an attempt to come to grips with some of those problems within the revolutionary movement I most closely identified and worked with, the Sandinistas. But rather than seeing the new social movements of the last two decades in Latin America as something clearly separate from the armed struggle, it would be more accurate to see them as outgrowths of the same contradictions, impulses, and sometimes even organizational frameworks that have now come around full circle to confront the same question as the armed struggle: how, in their pursuit of specific and localized demands, to join together with other groups to take over and begin to transform the state, and how to begin to transform society from the state?

In a famous passage in a letter to his parents, Che Guevara likened himself to Don Quijote. But Don Quijote is notably both a hero and a fool. A more comprehensive rethinking of the armed struggle would have to involve a critique of the misconceptions, arrogance, and just plain foolishness often involved in both its theory and practice. Even so, with all its flaws and sometimes lethal illusions, the armed struggle revealed Latin

America in its most generous, creative, courageous, and diverse possibilities. Like the sixties in the United States, with which it was closely bound up, the promise of the armed struggle pointed to the possibility of a more generous, genuinely democratic, and egalitarian future. It did not fail because of its internal contradictions—although there were many—nor was it condemned to defeat from the start; it was *defeated* by what turned out to be in the end a stronger, more ruthless enemy.

The human cost of that defeat was high, and that is something that has been largely forgotten too. The number of people killed in the course of the Latin American armed struggle has to be measured not in the tens but in the hundreds of thousands. By a rough but I think conservative estimate, between 500,000 and 700,000 people were killed by armed violence in Latin America between 1959 and 1990. Most—90 percent or more—of these deaths were due to counterrevolutionary violence on the part of armies and police or right-wing paramilitary organizations, in an effort to reverse the tide of radicalization in the Americas (which included, of course, not only armed struggle but also electoral challenges like that of Allende and the Unidad Popular in Chile); but one has to include the casualties inflicted directly by the guerrilla groups too. Some 200,000 of these deaths are represented by Guatemala alone, where the struggle between the guerrillas and the army was particularly intense. But there were also very high levels of killing, in multiples of tens of thousands, in El Salvador, Nicaragua, Argentina, Colombia, Peru, and in multiples of thousands in Chile, Brazil, Venezuela, Bolivia, the Dominican Republic, Mexico, Haiti, and Uruguay, and in the hundreds in other countries, including Grenada, Puerto Rico, and the United States itself (mainly among indigenous, African American, and Hispanic groups). To these figures must be added the millions of others imprisoned, tortured, thrown out of work, dislocated from their villages and lands, or forced into exile.

This tremendous level of repression can serve to strengthen the argument of those, like Beatriz Sarlo or David Stoll, who view the armed struggle as a lethal folly whose price was paid by ordinary folk. But it can also suggest that there was a high level of actual or potential support for the armed struggle that was turned back only by repression in some cases of near genocidal proportions.

Whatever position one takes on the ultimate wisdom or folly of the armed struggle, it is clear that it must be remembered and represented historically, not as an epiphenomenon, but as a deeply agonistic yet also momentous phase of modern Latin American history. In my own view (and, like Sarlo, I write from the position of someone who sympathized with the armed struggle), it should be seen as a flawed and, in its ultimate defeat, a tragic enterprise, but also a brave and generous one, that had at its core much of what Latin America still wants and aspires to become. I don't think the task of remembering the armed struggle is an easy one—like trying to remember a dream; it recedes as you get closer to it. My generation—the generation of the sixties—is probably the last that can undertake this task in terms of personal memory or recollection. But, as I have noted here, it is often more inclined to see where we went wrong than what we did right. That is what I mean by the paradigm of disillusion in the representation of the armed struggle. But in a way, our disillusion has not been *thorough* enough. It has not worked through the melancholia of defeat. As a result, it leaves (or seeks to impose) a residual guilt that shades into an acceptance of, or identification with, the powers that be, which, as I argued in chapter 5, ends up being something like a Latin American version of the neoconservative turn in post-sixties U.S. culture. In that way, the paradigm of disillusion has not prepared us to accept that the possibility of radical change has opened up once again in the Americas, North and South.

The Subaltern and the State

The question of Latinamericanism is, ultimately, a question of the identity of the Latin American state. Yet the inadequacy of the existing state
is precisely the problem that the discourse of Latinamericanism places at
its center. Some years ago Ileana Rodríguez posed bluntly what she felt
was at stake in the project of Latin American subaltern studies as follows:
"Our choice as intellectuals is to make a declaration either in support of
statism (the nation-state and party politics) or on behalf of the subaltern.
We chose the subaltern."[1] I have been arguing in different ways throughout these chapters that this way of looking at the relation between the
subaltern and the state (which is broadly characteristic of postmodernist social theory generally) is too one-sided, and that we are in need of a
new paradigm. To be more specific, what happens when, as has been the
case with some of the governments of the marea rosada in Latin America,
subaltern or, to use the expression more in favor today, subaltern-popular
social movements originating well outside the parameters of the state and
formal politics (including the traditional parties of the Left), have "become the state," to borrow Ernesto Laclau's characterization, or have lent
themselves to political projects seeking to occupy the state?[2]

There are at least two ready answers to this question: one, the subaltern
is a "site" essentially outside the logic of the state; two, subaltern agency
necessarily must at some point or other pass through the state, and in
doing so will modify it. José Rabasa offers a version of the first, arguing
apropos the marea rosada in particular from the perspective of subaltern
studies that "it makes little sense to beg the question of a new kind of

state (kind, benevolent, democratic) when the state cannot be conceived outside its role of protecting and administering capital, whether in the mode of safeguarding international finance or in the mode of a socialist administration of capital."[3] I would like to suggest here an alternative that is *post*subalternist, "post" in the sense that it displaces the subalternist paradigm but is also a *consequence* of that paradigm in that it involves rethinking the nature of the state and of the "national-popular" from the perspectives opened up by subaltern studies.

Subaltern studies is, or at least began as, a form of Marxism, but it originated precisely in the context of the crisis of "actually existing socialism" and revolutionary nationalism in the 1980s. It would not be too much to say, I think, that the collapse of communism was, in turn, itself part of a more general loss of confidence in the efficacy of the state to order human life that also affected political thinking in the capitalist world. The most consequential expression of that loss of belief in the state was, of course, neoliberalism. But it could also be said to have had "left" forms (it is enough to mention the names of Foucault and Deleuze in this regard). Among these could be counted subaltern studies.

Like other forms of postmodernist social thought, subaltern studies privileges the activity of "social movements" functioning outside the parameters of the state and formal politics. The space or territoriality of that activity is sometimes said to be "civil society"; at other times, the idea of civil society itself, linked as it is to forms of colonial modernity, is problematized. In subaltern studies, the subaltern is conceptualized as that which is not only outside the state, but also constitutively *opposed* to the state in some sense or other. To the extent that the state and modernity are bound up with one another, subaltern agency is not only anti-statist but also anti*modern*, interruptive of the developmental narrative of the formation, evolution, and perfection of the state and civil society. If hegemony is understood, to recall Gramsci's definition, as the "moral and intellectual leadership of the nation"—that is, as a power that both interpellates and emanates from the state—then the subaltern must by definition be something like what Derrida means by the "supplement": a "remainder" that is left out of, or escapes from, hegemonic articulation. This is the basis for assuming a kind of "elective affinity" between subaltern studies and deconstruction that I discussed in chapter 3 apropos Alberto Moreiras's *The Exhaustion of Difference*. In a recent discussion of the relation between Latinamericanism and deconstruction that takes its inspiration partly from Moreiras, Gareth Williams restates the point: "What deconstruction wants is precisely to interrupt the constitution of hegemony—which is not that of the subaltern—in the name of a politics that is different from the relation hegemony-subalternity, constructed with the sole purpose of subordination."[4]

But is it inevitable that hegemony involves "subordination"? The subalternity/hegemony distinction seems to involve a confusion between what Gramsci understood by hegemony—that is, "leadership" as a discursively elaborated form of consensus or "persuasion" that can bring together heterogeneous social or class components into a "historical bloc"—and the more ordinary language sense of hegemony as domination or subordination, in the sense of the coercive imposition of the perspective of a particular class, group, or nation over others, as in, for example, the familiar phrase "U.S. hegemony." More precisely, the distinction confuses the *form* of hegemony—"moral and intellectual leadership"—with its content (both socialist-feminism and fascism are forms of hegemonic articulation, but obviously with quite different consequences).[5]

Moreover, the distinction governing/governed is not necessarily coterminous with the distinction hegemonic/subaltern. A government based on popular-subaltern hegemony would, it goes without saying, seek to subordinate the social classes or groups that are actually hegemonic and that express their hegemony through their control of both the state and the dominant institutions of civil society (including organized religion and education) and the economy. For example, in the Haitian Revolution the slave-owning planter class became a subordinated group, in the sense that its own identity and interests were coercively negated—its plantations were confiscated, and many of the slave owners and their families and associates were killed or forced into exile. Does that mean that the former slave owners became "subaltern"? In a narrow sense, yes, if—to recall Guha's definition—the subaltern is "a name for the general attribute of subordination . . . whether this is expressed in terms of class, caste, age, gender and office or in any other way," so that "in any other way" *could* be understood as including having one's slaves rebel and one's plantations seized. But to insist on that point (rather than, for example, to characterize the former slave owners as counterrevolutionary émigrés) would seem to distort significantly the meaning and political valence of the idea of the subaltern.[6]

Where, by contrast, one could speak meaningfully about the distinction between the state and the subaltern is in the relations of subordination that developed between the postrevolutionary state created by the Haitian Revolution and the population of former slaves that had generated the revolution "from below," so to speak, particularly around the question of restoring private property and labor discipline in plantation agriculture. Hegemony would represent here the pretension of a newly founded nation-state and its leaders (Toussaint, Dessalines, etc.) over those of its population. That conflict, *within* the revolution, so to speak, is one of the main—and ongoing—contradictions of Haitian history.[7] But it was not inevitable that the postrevolutionary state should have taken the form it did. That it did was the result of a "Thermidorian" reaction in the process of the revolution, which as in the case of the French Thermidor was brought on in part by economic blockade and foreign military threats against the new republic. One could imagine a different sort of state if the interests of the former slaves had prevailed.[8]

Or is it in the nature of all postrevolutionary states to institute a new regime of repression, so that the problem is the state itself (as in the neoliberal argument against historical communism)? Is there is always a Thermidor, a conservative reconciliation between the state and revolution? Is the state itself a form of coloniality of power (but then one would have to consider forms of the state that predate European colonialism, and indeed may persist beyond it)? On the other hand, it is clear that the (self-) emancipation of the slaves required a new state, whatever eventual form it might take (republican, monarchic, popular-democratic, "national," etc.). Without "becoming the state," the slaves would have remained in slavery.

I don't mean to minimize the distance that separates subalternity and the state (and the sphere of formal politics, parties, parliament, trade unions, etc.), because it is *precisely in the space* created by that distance that those new, and newly effective, forms of radical politics appear. As I noted before, the need for a criticism/self-criticism of leftist statism—including the countries of "actually existing socialism" and the modern states that originated from anticolonial struggles—was one of the driving forces behind the emergence of subaltern studies, which in a future direction was oriented to the possibility of new forms of popular-democratic political practice.[9] But, as I noted in my discussion of the relation between Latinamericanism and deconstruction, the deconstructive articulation of subaltern studies involves in effect a rejection of the political as such, and therefore of the possibility of political agency and creativity from subaltern-popular positions. In a sense, in the very act of enunciating subaltern positionality and declaring solidarity with it, it resubalternizes the political agency of the subaltern. To put this somewhat differently, to make the claim that deconstruction is on the side of the subaltern, whereas "hegemony" is on the side of domination, is precisely not to deconstruct the binary that grounds that claim in the first place.

The state itself is, of course, not one thing, but a shifting and complex field of relations.[10] So what it means to "have" state power is not always self-evident. How sovereign is even a highly centralized, authoritarian-populist government like Chávez's, when it does not exercise a monopoly on the means of violence, when the urban *turbas* that have been key supporters of the Bolivarian project are both inside and outside the state, and when Venezuela's economy continues to be crucially dependent on oil exports, and the space between the state and private enterprise is riddled with complex flows of national and international capital, involving among other things narcotraffic and "deals" and corruption at all levels?[11]

But that does not mean that it is *nothing* at all to have state power. Corruption, cronyism, and ideological posturing are nothing new in Venezuela. Nor would, I think, one want to say that the alternative to what one does not like about Chavismo would be "progressive" (or not) social movements operating outside the state versus a state (and a public sphere, including the media) controlled essentially by the Right and the ruling class—in other words, something like Venezuela was under a succession of governments beholden to neoliberal "structural adjustment" before Chávez. Chavismo was precisely the result of the crystallization of a variety of social movements operating in Venezuela in the wake of the Caracazo into a new political bloc. Despite the rhetoric of "twentieth-century socialism," Chávez's Venezuela is not socialism in any customary sense of that word. But it does keep alive the idea of socialism as the possibility of a postcapitalist order of things, and it does so in a way that still involves, by most accounts, an active relation, including elections and referenda, between the subaltern-popular sectors and the state.

Globalization has undoubtedly weakened in some ways the sovereignty of individual nation-states, and neoliberal policies have weakened in turn the bond between populations and states; but it is also now generally understood that the state continues to serve a necessary if (in some people's minds) transitional function within globalization.

Saskia Sassen has noted in this regard: "The nation-state remains the prevalent organizational source of authority and to variable extents the dominant one. But . . . critical components of authority deployed in the making of the territorial state are shifting toward becoming strong capabilities for detaching that authority from its exclusive territory and onto multiple bordering systems. Insofar as these systems are operating inside the nation-state, they may be obscuring the fact that a significant switch has happened."[12] Sassen speaks in particular of the "growing distance between the state and the citizen" induced by globalization, population diasporas, cybernetic networking, and privatization under neoliberal auspices, as entailing "the emergence of a new type of political subject that does not quite correspond to the notion of a formal political subject that is the voting and jury-serving citizen"; for example, indigenous movements that "go directly to international fora and bypass the nation-state" or legal cases based on international human rights law. "The multiplying of informal political subjects," she suggests, in seeming coincidence with subaltern studies, "points to the possibility that the excluded (in this case from the formal political apparatus) also can make history, thereby signaling the complexity of powerlessness" (321).

But it would be the promise of new forms of politics like Chavismo precisely to find ways to bring such a "new type of political subject" *into* politics. By the same token, the appeal beyond the nation-state to "international fora" has to have, at some point, both political support and concrete policy consequences within the nation-state. So the question of who controls the state — to the extent it means something to control the state — remains crucial to people's lives. At one level, this is simply a matter of saying that the Greens were wrong, it does make a difference whether you have a good cop or a bad cop, Obama or Bush. But, since most of us would agree that both Bush and Obama leave intact the status quo in terms of the distribution of both class and geopolitical power and wealth, for our concerns here, which are those of the politics of the "excluded," to recall Sassen's characterization above, the question of the state also involves what one might call its "transformative" possibility. That possibility has a double dimension: how the state itself can be radicalized and modified as a consequence of bringing into it demands, values, experiences from the popular-subaltern sectors (which would require a prior process of hegemonic articulation of a new political bloc capable of addressing the state), and how, in turn, *from* the state, society itself can be remade in a more redistributive, egalitarian, culturally diverse way (how hegemony might be constructed from the state, in other words).

What would it mean to simply renounce this double possibility on the assumption that the state is wholly bound up with domination and the maintenance and reproduction of capitalist relations of production and exchange? Let me consider the case of the Zapatistas, who were one of the social movements that the project of Latin American subaltern studies was most closely aligned with (Rabasa's argument against the marea rosada, cited earlier, is among other things a defense of both the Zapatista insurgency and its present political stance). It is well known that the Zapatistas, while they were willing to challenge the state militarily, refused, unlike the guerrilla movements of the 1960s and 1970s, to bid for state power, claiming that the space of their intervention was Mexican "civil society," and that they would "rule by obeying." True to that principle, they decided to stay out of the 2006 presidential elections in Mexico rather than give support to the campaign of the center-left political formation, the Partido de la Revolución Democrática (PRD), which promised something like a Mexican variant of the marea rosada, and which attracted, initially at least, widespread support and expectations. In retrospect, it seems clear that this decision contributed at least in some measure, in a way similar to what happened with the Greens in the 2000 election in the United States, to the PRD's failure to achieve an electoral majority—or, more probably, to producing a majority vote in favor of the PRD but one narrow enough to allow the election results to be manipulated so as to give the election to the Partido de Acción Nacional (PAN), as in the Florida results in 2000 in the United States. The Zapatista argument was that it was more important to further radicalize "civil society" in the direction of more fundamental change than to encourage people to participate in an election that involved what they considered a flawed reformist party—the PRD—and a deeply corrupt and repressive state apparatus.

Like the Greens apropos Gore, the Zapatistas did not expect or even *want* the PRD to lose. They looked rather to being an extraparliamentary "left opposition" to what would have been an inevitably highly contradictory center-left state project. As those contradictions developed, so would the force of the more radical position they represented. But the result did not leave the playing field the same as it was before the election, even for the Zapatistas. The PRD's loss left progressive forces in Mexico in general, whether they supported the PRD or not, discouraged and disoriented, since what had been expected, given the debilitating effects of neoliberal policies on the popular sectors in Mexico, was a PRD victory, and instead the country continued to be governed by a party, the PAN, identified more or less explicitly with neoliberalism. And it was not just a matter of the PAN's winning (or stealing) the election; once it was returned to power, it could also organize politically from the state against organizations of "civil society," most spectacularly if so far unsuccessfully against the drug cartels, of course, but also against trade unions, social movements, indigenous groups, and in many cases local activists of the PRD itself (as we have seen in the prolonged struggles in Oaxaca and Guerrero). The government could portray itself, in a society increasingly threatened—because of the very neoliberal policies the PAN propagated—by economic and social decomposition and organized crime, as the defender of law and order.

As is well known, the result has been a drop in electoral support for the PRD in the years following the 2006 elections, since it is no longer seen as a hegemonic alternative to the neoliberal state, and deep internal conflicts within the party, which have produced a series of splits. But it was not that the Zapatistas *gained* political authority or expanded their following in the meantime. It is rather the old, discredited Partido Revolucionario Institucional (PRI)—the party of the preneoliberal Mexican state—that has come to occupy the vacuum created by the PRD's unexpected loss and decline and the continued antipopular policies of the PAN. As in the case of the Greens in 2000, the Zapatistas' calculation that sitting out the election would strengthen the case for a radical alternative to the status quo turned against them too. The U.S. Greens have all but disappeared; the Zapatistas have not, but their influence and authority has certainly been contained. The PRD, deeply divided and far from enjoying anything close to a possible electoral majority, entered into a pact with the PAN to prevent a PRI landslide in the regional elections for state governors in the summer of 2010 by agreeing to support each other's candidates against the PRI candidate in some races. At the moment, the PRI is favored to win the presidential election scheduled in 2012.

The Zapatistas might say about this latest development, "I told you so." But the truth of that prophecy is a self-fulfilling one. Instead of making pacts with the PAN, the PRD should have been negotiating from the state with the Zapatistas (perhaps one or more of the ministers of a PRD government might have been a Zapatista), who in turn would be putting pressure on the PRD to live up to its electoral promises. That would have been a situation in which the "exteriority" of the Zapatistas would have had some force; now that exteriority is relatively meaningless and, in any case, easily contained by state and paramilitary counterinsurgency forces.

I would argue that there was a double theoretical error in the Zapatista decision to sit out the 2006 election that is similar to the error involved in the antistatist articulation of subaltern studies: (1) imagining that the state as such is, because of its historically material ties to colonialism and capitalism, outside the range of what counts as the exploited or subaltern or "the poor"; and (2) imagining that civil society is a space separate from the state and electoral politics, not seeing their relationship dialectically. This theoretical error, in turn, also resulted in a strategic *political* error, an error that was unwittingly complicit with the weakening of the Left in Mexico, the militarization of Mexican society, and the perpetuation of right-wing rule for the near future.[13]

Let me try to expand on what I think is involved here by contrasting two different formulations of the nature of the subaltern and of its political agency, or lack thereof. The first is from a 1993 essay by Gayatri Spivak that is representative, I think, of the antistatist articulation of subaltern studies I am concerned with. Spivak is writing here about the subaltern as a kind of limit of the nationalist project of the postcolonial state:

> Especially in a critique of metropolitan culture, the event of political independence can be automatically assumed to stand between colony and decolonization as an unexamined good that operates a reversal. But the political goals of the new nation are supposedly determined by a regulative logic derived from the old colony, with its interests reversed: secularism, democracy, socialism, nationalist identity, and capitalist development. Whatever the face of this supposition, it must be admitted that there is always a space in the new nation that cannot share in the energy of this reversal. This space has no established agency of traffic with imperialism. Paradoxically, this space is also outside of organized labor, below the attempted reversals of capital logic. Conventionally, this space is described as the habitat of the subproletariat or the subaltern.[14]

The second formulation of the relation of the subaltern and the state is from an essay by Álvaro García Linera, "State Crisis and Popular Power," published in translation in 2006 in the *New Left Review*, just after he took office as vice president in the MAS (Movimiento al Socialismo) government in Bolivia (although the writing of the essay both predates and anticipates the MAS victory by some years). García Linera writes:

> The important thing to note about these popular groupings, hitherto excluded from decision making [García Linera is referring to indigenous communities, retirees, coca-growing peasants, unemployed miners or *relocalizados*, among other new social movements in Bolivia], is that the demands they raise immediately seek to modify economic relations. Thus their recognition as a collective political force necessarily implies a radical transformation of the dominant state form, built on the marginalization and atomization of the urban and rural working classes. Moreover—and this is a crucial aspect of the current reconfiguration—the leaderships of these new forces are predominantly indigenous, and uphold a specific cultural and political project. In contrast to the period that opened with the 1930s when the social movements were articulated around a labour unionism that held to the ideal of mestizaje—or racial-cultural mixing—and was the result of an economic modernization carried out by business elites, today the social movements with the greatest power to interrogate the political order have an indigenous social base, and spring from agrarian zones excluded from or marginalized by the processes of economic modernization.[15]

A moment's reflection will suffice to establish that Spivak and García Linera are talking about the *same* thing here: the social groups left out or only partially incorporated ("excluded from decision making"; "below the attempted reversals of capital logic") by the postcolonial nation-state's project of modernization and secularization—and in similar ways. That is, the "subaltern." Yet the logic of their arguments is strikingly different. In Spivak, the subaltern is a "space" or "habitat" that is *outside* of the nationalist articulation of the postcolonial state and the sphere of politics or trade union struggle—that is, outside of (or below) hegemony. The subaltern cannot speak. The task of the critical intellectual is to represent, or "read," to use Spivak's own term, this constitutive dilemma, and to lend one's solidarity in what is essentially an ethical gesture.[16] For García Linera, by contrast, the very logic of the demands of the social movements or "popular groupings" lead them "necessarily"—his own characterization—to pose the question of "a radical transformation of the dominant state form." Whether those demands take an electoral or an insurrectionary form (García Linera allows for both), they must create a new form of hegemony. The subaltern can not only speak, it can and should govern, and its form of government will be a "buen gobierno."[17]

García Linera invokes explicitly Gramsci's definition of hegemony in this regard: "This indigenous-popular pole should consolidate its hegemony, providing intellectual and moral leadership of the country's social majorities. There will be neither electoral triumph nor victorious insurrection without wide-ranging, patient work on the unification of the social movements, and a practical education process to realize the political, moral, cultural and organizational leadership of these forces over Bolivia's popular and middle strata" (83). The task of the "traditional" intellectual—and García Linera is himself one (he was trained as a mathematician)—is not to assume exclusively the authority to create "intellectual and moral leadership" but to lend himself or herself to a process whose main articulating agent is "the indigenous-popular pole." This involves a *political* rather than, as in Spivak, a primarily *ethical* relation of solidarity between intellectuals and subaltern social classes and groups.

García Linera argues for a new form of politics directed at "becoming" the state that in some sense comes *from* the subaltern, but also involves the participation of intellectuals and "theory." He moves away from the simple binary opposition between the state and the subaltern, to presuppose that hegemony not only can be but needs to be constructed from subaltern positions. This is, of course, not only a theoretical proposition (although it is that). It was implicated in the formation and subsequent activity of the Bolivian MAS. It involves in that regard at least four forms of strategic political articulation: (1) an openness to both insurrectional and electoral forms of political struggle, or some combination of both at the same time, as was the case in Bolivia in the period between 2000 and the 2005 election (García Linera himself spent several years in jail in the 1990s for "subversive" activities); (2) the identification of an enemy: the "dominant state form," "economic modernization carried out by business elites," "the ideal of mestizaje"; (3) a "specific" indigenous cultural and political project—that is, the affirmation of an ethnic identity and corresponding forms of language, worldview, and social organization; and (4) a sense of the need for "leadership," but leadership exercised *by* and *from* rather than in the name of the "indigenous-popular pole."

We might, in a kind of shorthand, call these forms of articulation "Schmittian."[18] But the contrast between these formulations by Spivak and García Linera does not necessarily come down to an either/or choice.

They could be seen instead to represent different forms of strategic inter-vention and ideological articulation that might be relevant in different forms of territoriality or levels of the social: one for transnational human rights organizations, NGOs, ecological struggles, the "global" humanities itself; the other in a space still conceived more narrowly as "national," though not closed to international issues. There will be points of contra-diction (for example, between the demands of indigenous movements and the imperatives of territorial sovereignty and economic develop-ment). However, the effects of intervention on either level need not always be antithetical, and could instead be mutually reinforcing in some cases.

Spivak has spoken herself of "*reinventing* the state." For example (this is from a 2004 interview):

> The more geopolitical stuff can work *only if* in the global south, we re-invent the state as an abstract structure, as a porous abstract structure, so that states can combine against the deprivations of internationalization through economic 'restructuring.' . . . Nobody looks at the possible effi-cacy of state structures because people have their faith today in everything outside governments. Remember, I'm not talking about national sover-eignty, I'm talking about abstract state structures that are porous. I'm talk-ing about critical regionalism, shared laws, shared health, education, and welfare structures, open frontiers rather than only economic organiza-tions. . . . Otherwise, to give accountability over to nongovernmental orga-nizations [NGOs]—I don't think nongovernmental organizations should be abolished—can become a way of letting organizations like the USAID [United States Agency for International Development] into a country. . . . The World Bank is an NGO after all. Giving over all accountability to this group, which then conspires against the individual states and sees them only as areas of repression is also to take power away from citizens who can after all supposedly *make* the state accountable.[19]

Still, what Spivak means by "reinventing the state" here, despite the point about the "possible efficacy of state structures," seems quite different than what is entailed in the MAS project of winning national elections and cre-ating a "plurinational" Bolivian state. Spivak puts her remarks under the rubric of a "position without identity," including national identity: "I'm not talking about national sovereignty" (245). "I know that something has to be counterposed to the main outposts of power. On the other hand, I am deeply troubled by identity politics, so for me it cannot be India, it cannot be Bengal, as a political basis for a problematic" (240). "There is much talk these days of the emergence of subaltern counter-collectivity. I think that is bogus. If you nominate collectivities that are questioning the power of the United States or the power of the West or whatever as immediately a subaltern counter-collectivity, I don't think you really know what it is like where this conflict *can mean nothing*" (247).

The place where "this conflict *can mean nothing*" thus continues to be for Spivak, as in her 1993 comments cited previously, the space designated by the subaltern, whereas the kind of "indigenous-popular" political bloc imagined by García Linera is precisely a form of subaltern "countercollectivity" that involves at its core cultural and national "identity," both at the group (indigenous cultural affirmation) and the national level (anti-imperialist nationalism).

Spivak's appeal to the state as an "abstract" porous structure paradoxically ends up leaving the character of the existing state mechanisms intact. By contrast, the MAS project involves not only political control of the state by a popular-subaltern block, but also its transformation. But that project/prospect raises both in theory and practice a number of urgent and difficult questions, some of which we have already anticipated in the previous discussion. For example, in the case of governments like the MAS or the Correa regime in Ecuador that have a strong indigenous and Afro-Latin component, is there the danger of a fracture between the the goals of the ethnic movements as such and the broader hegemonic bloc precisely around "reasons of state" (for example, on issues related to the exploitation of energy resources) ? How can that fracture be avoided or mediated? What happens to the state—still marked institutionally in many ways by coloniality of power—as the consequence of a subaltern-popular agency within it? What is the place of multiculturalism—or to use the term preferred in Latin America, interculturalidad—in the redefinition of the identity of the nation-state (the point of the distinction is to mark an alternative to a sort of "weak" multiculturalism coterminous with neoliberal hegemony)? What new constitutional-rights forms of legal and political territoriality are required by a "multinational state"? What should be the relation of formal or informal social movements to the new governments of the marea rosada they have helped bring to power? Do the social movements capture the state, or are they instead captured by it, limiting the radical force and possibility they carried initially, such that, to recall Antonio Negri's distinction, they belong to the side of constituted rather than constituent power? It is sobering to consider that, as of this writing, *all* of these potential points of contradiction and conflict have appeared within the project of the Bolivian MAS, and moreover seem to be taking the form in particular of a growing split between García Linera himself and intellectuals and activists more closely bound up with the demands of the indigenous movements. So the contrast I have drawn here between Spivak and García Linera is intended more in the nature of what Cervantes called a "novela ejemplar," a cautionary tale that mixes a skeptical realism with hope. Hope for what? Does the possibility of socialism reappear again with the marea rosada, after the historical collapse and defeat of the communist project in the twentieth century, or are the horizons represented by the new governments of the Left in Latin America limited to reformist strategies, strategies that respect and leave intact in the last instance the structure of both national and global market capitalism, as Rabasa argues? What then about the "withering away" of the state?

García Linera responds to this last—and perhaps most decisive— question in the following way:

> The general horizon of the era is communist. And this communism will have to be constructed on the basis of society's self-organizing capacities, of processes for the generation and distribution of communitarian, self-managing wealth. But at the moment it is clear that this is not an immediate horizon, which centers on the conquest of equality, the redistribution of wealth, the broadening of rights. . . . When I enter into the government, what I do is to validate and begin to operate at the level of the State in function of this reading of the current moment. So then, what about communism? What can be done from the State in function of this communist horizon? To support as much as possible the unfolding of society's autonomous organizational capacities. This is as far as the possibility can go in terms of what a leftist State, a revolutionary State, can do.[20]

With these words (and the debate around García Linera himself in the project of the MAS) in mind, let me return to the question I began with: Does the critique of the state in subaltern studies and postmodernist social theory generally rule out in advance the possibility of occupying and transforming the state from subaltern-popular positions? If the answer is yes, this possibility is in fact ruled out, then it seems that two alternatives remain: one is neoconservative, the other ultraleftist. As I suggested in chapter 5, the neoconservative alternative points in the direction of a reterritorialization of the field of culture and national identity against what are seen as the debilitating effects of neoliberalism, via a strengthening of the state ideological apparatuses, particularly education (an affirmation of the national culture, aesthetic and scientific "value," the authority of the academic disciplines, the role of the critical intellectual and of professionals, etc.). Hegemony implies here essentially the reassertion of the authority of the educated classes and technical-professional intelligentsia—the contemporary version of Ángel Rama's "lettered city" or *ciudad letrada*—to govern responsibly in the name of the "people" and in the interests of the "nation" in globalization. As in the case of some forms of U.S. neoconservatism, such a reterritorialization of authority at the level of the cultural and the political is not necessarily incompatible with a strong Keynesian or social democratic economic policy. In that sense, the neoconservative turn, in the form of a neo-Arielism, could be and in fact often is a component of the new governments of the Left. But this is at the risk of reinscribing or deepening a line of difference with the subaltern-popular sectors those governments depend on for their support.

The neoconservative move involves an emphasis on the state *over* the subaltern, the intelligentsia over the "people." The ultraleftist move, rooted in part in subaltern and postcolonial studies, is, by contrast, anti-statist and postnationalist. Something like that possibility is represented by Hardt's and Negri's *Empire*, which we have already considered at some length in chapter 2. To recall briefly their argument: For Hardt and Negri, economic globalization represents a new stage of capitalism with its own special characteristics. In this stage, the nation-state, which had been the territorial form that corresponded to the previous stages of capitalism (mercantile, competitive, and monopoly), is now surpassed. The new revolutionary subject—the "multitude"—is therefore necessarily postnational or transnational, hybrid, and diasporic. The emergence of the sovereign nation-state in early modernity was already an imposition on the autonomy of the multitude. Now, the power of the multitude will reassert itself. Indeed, that power is immanent in the very movement of globalization. As I noted in my introduction, the book that comes closest, in my mind, to expressing a vision of Latinamericanism coincident with the perspective of Hardt and Negri is Jon Beasley-Murray's *Posthegemony* (2010). (I should add, however, that Beasley-Murray explicitly separates his argument from Hardt's and Negri's somewhat millenarian claim that the possibility of a new form of communism is immanent in the contemporary capitalist order of things. Negri himself addresses the question of Latin America in a volume of conversations with Giuseppe Cocco, *Global: Bipoder y luchas en una América Latina globalizada*, published in 2006.)

Paradoxically, both the neoconservative "turn" I sketched in chapter 5 and the discourse of the "multitude" or "posthegemony" coincide in expressing a skepticism about or an outright rejection of the new governments of the marea rosada in Latin America, particularly those with a more "populist" character, such as Chávez in Venezuela. By contrast, in my remarks here I am aligning myself in some ways with those governments. Although they are each vitally concerned with reasserting national sovereignty, their project involves not simply rearticulating the nation-state as it was prior to globalization and neoliberalism. For one thing, it is not possible for them to delink the question of sovereignty from a regional affirmation of Latin America as a transnational entity, that is, as what Samuel Huntington understands by the idea of a "civilization." That is why the problematic of "Latin America" appears in their geopolitical articulation in the first place, otherwise they would remain centered simply on their respective national interests. (Chávez's Bolivianism is not only rhetorical. He has on more than one occasion put his money where his mouth is to promote new forms of Latin American unity at both the economic and cultural levels.)

The challenge that confronts the marea rosada if it is to move forward rather than recede is to generate, first, the idea and, second, the institutional forms of a different state, a state that would, under the conditions of globalization, embody and express the egalitarian, democratic, multicultural, multiethnic character of the "people": a people-state, or a state *of* the people. I intend by the idea of a people-state to mark a distinction between a state whose character would be defined by horizontal relations between state representatives and functionaries and the "people," and therefore also by "contradictions among the people," and a *populist* state characterized by vertical relations between leaders/the leader and the people and by the suppression of "contradictions among the people" in the name of national unity, with the understanding, however, that it is not always easy to hold the two things apart, as in the case of Chávez.

García Linera has spoken of "a state that is not a state."[21] Would this new form of the state continue to be a *nation*-state, however? That is, a state founded on the idea of a certain shared "national identity" and a contiguous territoriality that is expressive of that identity? Yes and no. This final question brings to the fore again the issue that has been present since the beginning of this book. Jorge Volpi and Michael Hardt and Antonio Negri (on nominally opposite sides of the political spectrum) are wrong. The Latin American nation-states and "Latin America" as a transnational entity will continue to exist and to exercise a certain "hegemony" over people's lives. But they will do so in radically new ways, which we have only begun to anticipate and understand.

Notes

INTRODUCTION

This book is based on a group of interrelated essays about the relation of Latin American cultural theory and poltics that I wrote between 2002 and 2009. I have revised all of them, so they differ, sometimes substantially, from previously published versions in both Spanish and English.

1. Santí, "Latinamericanism and Restitution," *Latin American Literary Review* 40 (1992): 88–96; "Sor Juana, Octavio Paz, and the Poetics of Restitution," *Indiana Journal of Hispanic Languages* 1.2 (1993): 101–39. Both are reprinted in Santí, *Ciphers of History*, which I use as a reference here.

2. De la Campa, *Latin Americanism*, vii.

3. Moreiras, *The Exhaustion of Difference*, 1. Elsewhere, he writes: "Latin Americanism is university discourse: the conflicted discourse of the principle of reason concerning Latin America."

4. Castro-Goméz and Mendieta, *Teorías sin disciplina.*

5. The proceedings are in Beasley-Murray, *Towards a New Latin Americanism.*

6. "Latin-Americanism at least as practiced in humanistic disciplines within the North American university exists today as a strange kind of ritualized enclave, outwardly cosmopolitan, but, beneath the surface, increasingly provincial and sectarian. It has become a form of 'study' that, over the last couple of decades, has succeeded in inventing for itself a theoretically 'regional' object with almost no remaining connection to any real place" (Larsen, "Latin-Americanism without Latin America," 37).

7. Mendieta, "Remapping Latin American Studies," 287. One might, in turn, pluralize each of these Latinamericanisms by adding those of indigenous peoples, Afro-Latinos, women, Latin American Jews and Muslims, LGBTs, and others.

8. Santí speaks of "the stand of most Liberal Latinamericanists, both in Europe

and the United States, whose implicit sympathy for the material plight of the people in whose countries provides a moral justification for their work," adding that he doubts that such "sympathy by itself would be enough to bypass the snares of as entrenched a discourse as *Latinamericanism,* or that simply by expressing lofty platitudes a Liberal European can neutralize the paternalism implicit in his perception of so-called *Latinamericans*" (*Ciphers,* 222).

9. Most immediately through Geoffrey Hartmann's essay, on "the restoration of voice to mute classes of people" (that is, on testimony and *testimonio*), "The Philomela Project," 164–75, which provides Santí with his notion of the relation between criticism and restitution. Santí also mentions Spivak's "Can the Subaltern Speak?" in this regard.

10. Paul de Man himself noted (apropos Rousseau): "To the extent that it is necessarily misleading, language just as necessarily conveys the promise of its own truth. This is why textual allegories on this level of textual complexity generate history" (*Allegories of Reading,* 277).

11. Laclau, "Deriva populista y centroizquierda latinoamericana."

12. My friend and former colleague in the Latin American Subaltern Studies Group, José Rabasa, instructs that "we must stop feeling complacent about the return of the Left in Latin America," arguing that "the new constitutions are precisely that—forms of constituted power that safeguard the interests of a ruling class" (Rabasa, "Exception to the Political," in his *Without History,* 251). I will come back to Rabasa's argument, which seems to me like a contemporary version of what Lenin called "ultraleftism," in my final chapter, "The Subaltern and the State."

13. The constitutional referendum sponsored by the Movimiento al Socialismo (MAS) that passed in 2009 redefined Bolivia as an "Estado Plurinacional"—a plurinational state.

14. Barragán and Rivera Cusicanqui, *Debates post coloniales.*

15. Castañeda, "Morning in Latin America." The well-known Venezuelan journalist (and former guerrilla combatant) Teodoro Petkoff offered an earlier version of this idea.

16. Most observers of Latin America today would draw attention to China as a decisive new factor in the region, which in a way involves another form of South-South dialogue. China senses that a vacuum of hegemony has emerged in Latin America, and is stepping in to fill this vacuum. Where Castañeda argues for a U.S. policy that "fortifies the modern left, and weakens the retrograde left," inviting in this way continued confrontation of the United States with major actors and constituencies in Latin America, China, notably, has not been guided in its approach to Latin America by this dichotomy, or its underlying assumptions about regional economic integration under U.S. auspices, precisely because it would like to break open that framework in some ways. It is in the process of deepening its economic, cultural, and political relations with all governments in Latin America, including

especially those of the "retrograde Left" (with which it may feel a certain affinity, because of its own modern history and political character).

17. I am indebted to my colleague Gerry Martin for bringing Volpi's book to my attention.

18. Volpi's novel *El fin de la locura*, which is about the French 1968 rising and its aftermath, seen through the eyes of a Latin American intellectual living in Paris, is in some ways a postmodernist (and postleftist) version of Flaubert's *Sentimental Education*.

19. "The overlap of parallel social systems in the same physical space has given rise to acculturation in reverse — a process by which foreign customs, institutions, and language are diffused within the native population. As a consequence, biculturalism has emerged as an alternative adaptive project to full assimilation into American culture" (Portes and Stepick, *City on the Edge*, 8).

CHAPTER ONE: LATINAMERICANISM AFTER 9/11

This chapter is a translation and revision of an essay that originally appeared in Spanish as "El latinoamericanismo después de '9/11,'" *Casa de las Américas* 241 (October–December 2005): 132–37.

1. Hegel, *The Philosophy of History*, 86.

2. I hasten to add that I do not mean to suggest that Latin American states, individually or collectively, have or can have in the immediate future the means to confront the United States militarily. But I do think that Latin America collectively needs to be able to assure its territorial sovereignty vis-à-vis the United States, something it has been unable to do since 1848, and probably does have the means to ensure at least military détente with the United States, if that were to be posed as a strategic goal. Instead, Latin American militaries in general continue to be complicit with the U.S.-inspired drug eradication programs and U.S.-run training schools for police and officers, and remain focused on controlling their own populations rather than deterring external aggression (the campaign of the Cardenas government in Mexico against the drug cartels is one such case, and leaves Mexico open to increasing intervention by U.S. intelligence, police, and military forces). This situation has not changed with the advent of the Obama administration, which signaled its intentions by countenancing de facto the military coup in Honduras and mandating the expansion of U.S. military bases in Colombia, with the clear intention of pressuring the neighboring states, especially Venezuela, Ecuador, and Bolivia.

3. Huntington, *The Clash of Civilizations*.

4. Huntington recounts the following anecdote in *The Clash of Civilizations*: "In 1991 a top adviser to President Carlos Salinas de Gotari described at length to me all the changes the Salinas government was making. When he finished, I remarked: 'That's most impressive. It seems to me that basically you want to change Mexico from a Latin American country into a North American country.'

He looked at me with surprise and exclaimed: 'Exactly! That's precisely what we are trying to do, but of course we could never say so publicly'" (51).

5. See the classic study by Ardao, *Genesis de la idea y el nombre de América Latina*.

6. See my remarks in the introduction on Enrico Mario Santí's construction of the idea of Latinamericanism as the "interested" discourse of the Euro-American academy about Latin America.

7. Moraña, "El *boom* del subalterno."

8. It is interesting to note that the aversion to U.S.-associated forms of theoretical practice is generally not matched by the Latin American neo-Arielists with a parallel rejection of Western European—and particularly German and French—thought. To cite one example: Beatriz Sarlo takes some pains to differentiate British cultural studies—Raymond Williams and Stuart Hall—from the "bad" U.S. kind, in her essay "Raymond Williams: Una relectura." The neo-Arielists share this move of seeking a European or "classical" warrant against the "material" force and vulgarity of U.S. culture with Rodó and the *modernistas*.

9. García Canclini, *Consumidores y ciudadanos*.

10. I owe this idea to Haroldo Dilla.

11. I allude to the idea expressed by the Austro-Marxist Otto Bauer, *The Question of Nationalities and Social Democracy*. I will return to Bauer on the question of the nation in chapter 2. Bolivia now officially designates itself as a plurinational state, "Estado Plurinacional." But Bauer's idea of a multinational state might also extend to the articulation of Latin American states as a group in some form of regional federalism similar to what Bolívar envisioned.

12. Hegel, by contrast, sees in the passage I cited above the destruction of the peasantry and open lands as the precondition for the emergence of a modern state and civil society. For a more hopeful assessment of the marea rosada, see Emir Sader, *The New Mole*.

13. The Latinamericanist discourse of cultural *mestizaje* or transculturation which posits that Latin America has achieved a form of "racial democracy" distinct from the racial divide in the United States, is not in itself a mestizo discourse. While it is certainly more affirmative of non-European racial elements than extreme forms of U.S. racism, it also involves in some ways a mystification or covering up of the actual forms of racism that mestizos, as well as indigenous and Afro-Latin populations, continue to confront in Latin America.

CHAPTER TWO: THE PERSISTENCE OF THE NATION (AGAINST *EMPIRE*)

This chapter has its roots in a somewhat different essay, "Queering the Nation: Some Thoughts on Empire, Nationalism, and Multiculturalism Today," in Begoña Aretxaga, Dennis Dworkin, Joseba Gabilondo, and Joseba Zulaika, eds., *Empire and Terror: Nationalism/Postnationalism in the New Millennium* (Reno: University of Nevada/Center for Basque Studies, 2004): 79–92.

1. Hardt and Negri, *Empire*.

2. See, e.g., Hardt and Negri, "Antimodernity as Resistance," in the concluding volume of the "Empire" triology, *Commonwealth*, 67–82.

3. "The encounter between South Asian subaltern studies and Latin American critiques of modernity and colonialism have one thing in common: their conception that subalternity is not only a question of social groups dominated by other social groups, but of the subalternity in the global order, in the interstate system analyzed by Guha and by Quijano. Dependency theory was clearly an early reaction to this problematic. This is no doubt a crucial and relevant point today, when coloniality of power and subalternity are being rearticulated in a postcolonial and postnational period controlled by transnational corporations and by the network society" (Mignolo, "Coloniality of Power and Subalternity," 441).

4. Guha, "Preface," 35.

5. "I use the term *Exodus* here to define mass defection from the State. . . . Exodus is the foundation of a Republic. The very idea of 'republic,' however, requires a taking leave of State judicature: if Republic, then no longer State. The political action of Exodus consists, therefore, in an *engaged withdrawal*. Only those who own a way of exit for themselves can do the founding; but, by the opposite token, only those who do the founding will succeed in finding the parting of the waters by which they will be able to leave Egypt" (Virno, "Virtuosity and Revolution," 196).

6. Nimni, in Bauer, *The Question of Nationalities and Social Democracy*. Hardt and Negri take up Bauer in order to refute him: e.g., "In the gentle intellectual climate of that 'return to Kant,' these professors, such as Otto Bauer, insisted on the necessity of considering nationality a fundamental element of modernization. In fact, they believed that from the confrontation between nationality (defined as community of character) and capitalist development (understood as society) there would emerge a dialectic that in its unfolding would eventually favor the proletariat. This program ignored the fact that the concept of the nation-state is not divisible but rather organic, not transcendental but transcendent, and even in its transcendence it is constructed to oppose every tendency on the part of the proletariat to reappropriate social spaces and social wealth. . . . The authors celebrated the nation without wanting to pay the price of this celebration. Or better, they celebrated it while mystifying the destructive power of the concept of nation. Given this perspective, support for the imperialist projects and inter-imperialist war were really logical and inevitable positions for social-democratic reformism" (*Empire*, 111–12). Hardt and Negri are alluding here, of course, to the support of social democratic parties for the war aims in their respective countries in the First World War. But they confuse here Bauer's concept of the nation as a "multinational state" with Kautsky's, which was precisely the one taken over by Lenin and the Bolsheviks to defend "national liberation struggle." See, e.g., Nimni, *Marxism and Nationalism*.

7. Chakrabarty, *Provincializing Europe*, 95.

8. "The bibliography on culture tends to assume that there is an intrinsic interest on the part of the hegemonic sectors to promote modernity and a fatal destiny on the part of the popular sectors that keeps them rooted in tradition. From this opposition, modernizers draw the moral that their interest in the advances and promises of history justifies their hegemonic position: meanwhile, the backwardness of the popular classes condemns them to subalternity. . . . [But] traditionalism is today a trend in many hegemonic social layers and can be combined with the modern, almost without conflict, when the exaltation of traditions is limited to culture, whereas modernization specializes in the social and economic. It must now be asked in what sense and to what ends the popular sectors [also] adhere to modernity, search for it, and mix it with their traditions" (García Canclini, *Hybrid Cultures*, 145–46).

9. See Jameson's essay on the Soviet film director Tarkovsky, "On Soviet Magic Realism," in *The Geopolitical Aesthetic*.

10. Brown, *State of Injury*, 73–74.

11. Brown notes that identity politics, paradoxically (because its claims are often anti-Eurocentric), runs the risk of becoming "a protest that . . . reinstalls the humanist ideal so far as it premises itself on exclusion from it" (*State of Injury*, 65). For an articulation of "identity" that goes beyond the kind of conventional "identity politics" Brown critiques, without however abandoning the force of (subaltern) identity as a point of departure for emancipatory practices, including new forms of national or postnational territoriality, see Jerome Branche's *Malungaje* (2009).

CHAPTER THREE: DECONSTRUCTION AND LATINAMERICANISM

Part of this chapter derives from a review essay, "Beyond the Third Space," *Postcolonial Studies* 5.3 (2002): 327–32.

1. Moreiras develops and in some ways revises his position in a subsequent book, *Línea de sombra*, written post-9/11 and after the breakup of the Latin American Subaltern Studies Group, which he was affiliated with. I will take up *Línea de sombra* briefly in the conclusion to this chapter.

2. Román de la Campa anticipates this point in his book *Latin Americanism*, mentioned in the introduction. He notes there: "My purpose is not to turn literary deconstruction into a bête noire, or deny its momentous impact, but rather to behold its own set of taboos and traverse its unsuspected blind spots within Latin Americanism" (viii). There are many ways I find myself simply repeating this gesture here. But I should also note that de la Campa's critique is more centered on "postmodernism" than on deconstruction per se, and it comes well before *The Exhaustion of Difference*, which in some ways could be seen as a response to *Latin Americanism*.

3. Jenckes, "The 'New Latin Americanism,' and the End of Regionalist Thinking?" Jenckes notes that she derives the phrase from the title of a conference held

at the University of Manchester on June 21–22, 2002, organized by Jon Beasley-Murray and Patience Schell. Some of the papers from the Manchester conference were published in a special issue of the *Journal of Latin American Cultural Studies* 11.3 (2002). See also the special issue of *South Atlantic Quarterly* 106.1 (2007), *Latin America: In Theory*, edited by David Johnson.

4. Santí is particularly explicit, and scornful on this score: "The Liberal rhetoric of sympathy or salvation, often couched in mindless platitudes, is but one more and ever so powerful turn in the attempt to position the European in a superior relation to non-European peoples and cultures. Such 'noble' efforts often work to reinforce, rather than dispel, the oppressive discourse of *Latinamericanism*. To paraphrase the Venezuelan essayist Carlos Rangel: if we once had a 'noble savage,' why could we not have now a 'noble revolutionary'?" (*Ciphers of History*, 222). The allusion is to the title of Rangel's book—one of the first to anticipate a postleftist, neoconservative turn in Latin American thought—*Del buen salvaje al buen revolucionario* (1967).

5. Idelber Avelar's study of Latin American postdictatorial narrative, *The Untimely Present*, appears the same year (1999) as *Tercer espacio* and shares a similar concern: how to develop a thinking of "resistance" from the ruins of the project of the Left under conditions of state terrorism and neoliberal hegemony.

6. David Stoll's attack in his 1999 book, *Rigoberta Menchú and the Story of All Poor Guatemalans*, on the veracity of Rigoberta Menchú's testimony, and the authority of what he called there "postmodernist anthropology," which Moreiras takes up briefly in *The Exhaustion of Difference*, represents one form of the response of the "hard" social sciences against the intrusion of literary and cultural theory. The progress of the conservative restoration in the 1990s in particular can be measured almost exactly by the degree to which "interdisciplinarity" becomes an increasingly combatted space or empty slogan in professional organizations like the Latin American Studies Association.

7. "A word is in order about a particular switch of focus that happens in the book between Parts One and Two. The first part draws more from historical and ethnographic studies of peasants and tribals, groups one could call 'subaltern' in a straightforward or sociological sense. The second part of the book concentrates on the history of educated Bengalis, a group which, in the context of Indian history, has often been described (sometimes inaccurately) as 'elite'" (Chakrabarty, *Provincializing Europe*, 19).

8. A similar idealization of literary culture, in this case of Hindu classical culture, is evident in Ranajit Guha's later writings, for example, his lectures on Hegel and the philosophy of history in *History at the Limit of World-History*. It appears that when South Asian subaltern studies is in dialogue with the Anglo-European academy and Orientalism, the classical cultural heritage of the Indian subcontinent is "resistant"; but when it is in dialogue with the nationalist historiography of its own countries, as in, for example, the opening chapter, "Negation," of Guha's

Elementary Aspects of Peasant Insurgency in Colonial India, that heritage is problematic, since it constitutes one of the grounds of subalternity (literacy/illiteracy) internal to those countries, with or without the experience of colonialism.

9. Both *The Exhaustion of Difference* and the later *Línea de sombra* engage centrally with Laclau, seeming at the same time to embrace and reject him.

10. Moreiras, "Irrupción y conservación en las Guerras Culturales." I quote the text as reproduced in Richard, *Debates críticos en América Latina*, 2:130.

11. Levinson, *The Ends of Literature*. Both Levinson and Moreiras echo, in turn, earlier arguments to the same effect by Djelal Kadir in his book *Questing Fictions*, or by González Echevarría in his notion of the Archive.

12. Moreiras uses the phrase "affective investment" in his discussion of Antonio Cornejo Polar's valedictory essay "Mestizaje e hibridez: Los riesgos de las metáforas." He observes that Cornejo's defense there of Spanish against English as the language of Latinamericanist reflection is "made ambiguous given the Latin American linguistic and cultural heterogeneity that Cornejo himself so masterfully theorized. In spite of that ambiguity, however, a heartfelt and poignant defense of the 'Nuestra América' tradition is at stake in Cornejo's remarks—and this affective investment equally marks [Mabel] Moraña's, [Hugo] Achugar's, and [Beatriz] Sarlo's texts (although not [Nelly] Richard's). It is certainly not to be dismissed on supposedly unemotional intellectual grounds given that emotion may be the very heart of the matter under discussion" (321, n. 7). I will come back to Cornejo's essay, as an instance of neo-Arielism, in the next chapter.

13. Moreiras is from Galicia, a region that has had a conflicted relation with "Spain" due, among other things, to its relative poverty and to the fact that its regional language is not Spanish. That conflicted relation has been expressed by sometimes violent forms of Galician nationalism, including Marxist-Leninist variants of the same. But, as far as I am aware Moreiras has not written about the "critical regionalism" that is pertinent to his Galician identity. Perhaps the closest he comes to this is in his essay on the Spanish political novel *Volver al mundo* (which has to do with an ETA-like nationalist guerrilla organization) in *Línea de sombra*.

14. Kusch, *Indigenous and Popular Thinking in América*, 115–23.

15. See the comments of Castillo, Galende, and Villalobos on *Línea de sombra*, and Moreiras's response, "Pantanillos ponzoñosos," 78–87.

16. Beasley-Murray, "Introduction: A User's Guide," *Posthegemony*, xiv–xv. The reference to Williams is to *The Other Side of the Popular*.

17. See *Línea de sombra*, 191–239, and especially Moreiras's explication of the Spanish novel *Volver al mundo*, 277–306, mentioned in an earlier note. The key text by Arendt in this regard is *On Violence* (1970), where she questions Benjamin's "Critique of Violence" for its disregard of the parliamentary democracy and "reformism" of the Weimar republic, which she feels opens the doors for fascism, noting the link between Benjamin and Carl Schmitt. Derrida echoes this idea in

his own critique of Benjamin and Schmitt in *Politics of Friendship*, a text that is paradigmatic for Moreiras's position in *Línea de sombra*. This is not the place to take this issue up with the attention it deserves, but it might be observed that it was perhaps the limitations of Weimar social democracy in a period of deep crisis, rather than its critique, that paved the way for the appearance of fascism. The issue is not unrelated to what is at stake politically in the present crisis in Europe and the United States.

18. I refer of course to Althusser's famous essay "Ideology and Ideological State Apparatuses." Moreiras would respond that the form of ideology *is* its content.

CHAPTER FOUR: BETWEEN ARIEL AND CALIBAN

1. Reati and Goméz Ocampo, "Académicos y *gringos malos*," 606. The authors credit an earlier essay on this same topic by Lucille Kerr, "Academic Relations and Latin American Fictions."

2. Richard, "Intersecting Latin America with Latin Americanism." See also her earlier essay, "Cultural Peripheries: Latin America and Postmodernist Decentering." Herself the recipient of a Rockefeller Foundation Humanities Institute grant, Richard understands that what complicates the assumption that one can speak "desde Latinoamérica" unproblematically is the fact that Latin America's knowledge about itself now passes in part through the North American and European academy, because of the diaspora of Latin American intellectuals provoked first by the military dictatorships of the 1960s and 1970s, and then the effects of neoliberal economic policies on the professional and middle classes in the 1980s and 1990s.

3. Taylor, "The Politics of Recognition."

4. Trigo's introductory essay, "The 1990s: Practices and Polemics within Latin American Cultural Studies," gives a good, though somewhat tendentious, summary of the Latin American reaction to "studies." A useful anthology, which includes a number of essays from a crucial moment in the debate in the late 1990s, is Castro-Goméz and Mendieta, *Teorías sin disciplina*. For a recent, self-consciously explicit articulation of the neo-Arielist position, see Rojo, *Las armas de las letras*. However, for me, as for many others, the most moving statement of this position was perhaps the late Antonio Cornejo Polar's valedictory essay, "Mestizaje e hibridez," with its anguished recognition of the fact that the hegemonic language of Latinamericanist discourse had become English rather than Spanish and thus of "el poco honroso final del hispanoamericanismo" (yet, paradoxically, Cornejo Polar's own work was concerned with deconstructing the idea of a linguistically or culturally homogeneous Peru).

5. Achúgar is alluding to Prospero's characterization of Caliban's speech as "gabble": "Hegel thought that theoretical discourse was impossible in the Americas. So, can 'Latin Americans' in Latin America have 'theory,' whether minor or major? . . . Isn't something similar happening in the dialogue between Latin

Americanists from the North and the South to what was happening in the dialogue between Prospero and Caliban. . . . Could it be that 'theoretical babbling' is the place that present Anglo-Saxon postcolonial discourse reserves for postcolonial discourse in other languages?" (Achúgar, "Local/Global Latinamericanisms," 670, 679, 684–85).

6. Aronna, *"Pueblos Enfermos,"* 117–18, 134.

7. Consider, for example, the following comment by Abril Trigo on the testimonio debate: *"Testimonio* offered an extraordinary alibi for the left metropolitan Latin Americanist to bypass the mediation of local (Latin American) intellectuals in order to establish direct political alliances with the ultimate subaltern subject (natives, Indians, women, civil society), and by doing so, reinstate his metropolitan position in a devalued and de-centered field [Latin American studies]. *Testimonio* was the Real for those metropolitan academics in search of a vanishing other, in complete disregard of the real epistemological, political, or literary status of testimonial writing in Latin America" ("The 1990s," 354).

8. Gloria Anzaldúa's *Borderlands*, despite its considerable originality, is a variation of Saldívar's strategy. For the other, or "Americanist" strategy, see the classic article by Yúdice and Flores, "Living Borders/Buscando América," which has spawned a veritable small industry of books and articles on the originality of U.S. Latino popular culture, including Flores's own *From Bomba to Hip-Hop*, or Cristina García's novel *Dreaming in Cuban*.

9. In the extensive menu of postmodern "identities," I have discovered one of my own: as a child born and raised for the first twelve years of my life in Latin America by WASP parents from the United States, I am a "third (or trans-) culture kid" or TCK. The concept has come to designate a person who has spent a significant period of his or her childhood in a country or countries other than the country of origin of his or her parents, and is thus obliged to integrate in his own personal identity elements of the culture of that country or countries and the country of origin of the parents. In other words, a TCK does not participate fully in either the national identity (including the linguistic identity) of his or her parents or that of the country or countries he or she was brought up in. The novelist Roberto Bolaño was a third culture kid (Chilean parents, but brought up in Mexico). So is Barack Obama (who spent a significant part of his childhood in Indonesia), something that surely underlines the "birther" controversy. My thanks to Gene Bell-Villada, also a TCK Latinamericanist, for bringing the concept to my attention.

CHAPTER FIVE: THE NEOCONSERVATIVE TURN

This chapter is loosely based on "The Neoconservative Turn in Latin American Literary and Cultural Criticism," *Journal of Latin American Cultural Studies* 17.1 (2008): 65–83.

1. The collection edited by Emil Volek, *Latin America Writes Back*, includes a

number of essays that represent aspects of what I am calling the neoconservative turn, including Volek's own.

2. While the neoconservative/neoliberal distinction is important for understanding the special character and circumstances of the Latin American "turn," which is explicitly antineoliberal and antipostmodernist, one should not make too much of it either. Neoconservatism is an ideology especially directed at the state and the state ideological apparatuses, including education. But neoliberalism, despite its pretense of being antistatist, also requires the state, and even, as in the case of Chile under Pinochet, a "strong" state, among other things to impose privatization and structural adjustment policies on sometimes reluctant populations and to protect private property. From a conservative or reactionary point of view, the ideal would be neoliberal hegemony over economic policy and neoconservative hegemony, with a strong emphasis on cultural nationalism, over cultural institutions, including the school system. In this sense, as in many others, the Pinochet dictatorship has served as a model for subsequent right-wing regimes like Thatcher's or G. W. Bush's. On the relationship between neoliberalism and neoconservatism, chapter 3, "The Neoliberal State," of Harvey's *A Brief History of Neoliberalism* is useful.

3. Though there was a strong anti-Stalinist, and frequently Trotskyist, strain among the New York Intellectuals, there was also a shift toward a neoconservative position on the part of some figures associated with the U.S. Communist Party, such as the historian Eugene Genovese, who shared with the New York Intellectuals a visceral dislike of the New Left and the counterculture. In Irving Kristol's often repeated (and somewhat racist) phrase, "A neoconservative is a liberal who has been mugged by reality."

4. For the record, I should note that *La articulación de las diferencias* was based on a doctoral dissertation that Morales completed under my direction at the University of Pittsburgh, and that it bears a preface by me that anticipates the argument I make below.

5. Stoll, *Rigoberta Menchú and the Story of All Poor Guatemalans*.

6. As a novelist and essayist in the 1970s and 1980s, Morales was closely identified with the Guatemalan revolutionary Left; his first book of literary criticism, *La ideología de la lucha armada*, was a study of the political poetry of the armed struggle in Central America. He is also the author of an autobiographical novel, or what he calls a "testinovela," *Los que se fueron por la libre*, based on his own experiences as a cadre in a small revolutionary group that was eventually expelled from the URNG (Unidad Revolucionaria Nacional Guatemalteca), the main coordinating organization of the armed struggle in Guatemala.

7. Rama, *Transculturación narrativa en América Latina*.

8. Morales provides the estimate that between 100 and 200 thousand indigenous people were killed in Guatemala between 1982 and 1984, and another million displaced from their homes (*La articulación de las diferencias*, 42).

9. For an overview of the issues involved that takes a position sharply contrary to Morales's, see del Valle, *Maya Nationalisms and Postcolonial Challenges in Guatemala.*

10. Moraña, "El *boom* del subalterno." I mentioned this essay in chapter 4 as an example of what I called there the neo-Arielist position. Moraña charges postcolonial and subaltern studies with a critical neoexoticism that represents the Latin American subject as pretheoretical, marginal, and "Calibanesque" in relation to metropolitan standards.

11. For a critique of the "ethical turn," see Bruno Bosteels, "The Ethical Superstition."

12. One might take issue with the "sino" in Moraña's phrase, however, because there is nothing "simple" about inverting binary essentialisms, particularly if you are at the bottom end of the pair.

13. Sarlo, "Los estudios culturales en la encrucijada valorativa."

14. This is not simply for Sarlo a question of formal elaboration versus unmediated experience, because Sarlo is also harsh about the hyperformalized film *Los rubios* by Albertina Carri, which attempts to reconstruct the director's memory of her parents, who were disappeared when she was three years old, during the Proceso. Sarlo sees Carri's film as a trafficking in "postmemory"—Marianne Hirsch's idea of the reconstruction by children of survivors of traumatic events like the Holocaust of the memory of that event in their own lives, even though they did not experience it directly themselves. Sarlo sees postmemory (and Carri's film) as a fundamentally narcissistic construct; for example: "La inflación teórica de la posmemoria se reduce asi en un almacén de banalidades personales legitimadas por los nuevos derechos de la subjetividad" (134) [The theoretical inflation of postmemory reduces itself to a kind of collection of personal banalities legitimized by the new rights of subjectivity]. Sarlo seems unaware, however, that Carri was herself directly affected by the Proceso as a child (she was present, for example, when her parents were captured, as she depicts in the film), so *Los rubios* is not strictly speaking a postmemory text, but a kind of testimonio. I owe this insight to Ana Forcinito.

15. See, for example, Sarlo's op-ed column on Kirchner in *La Nación.*

16. Sarlo, "Contra la mimesis."

17. Sarlo discussed the relation between intellectuals and Peronism directly (in part as a kind of self-criticism) in an essay that has been translated as "Intellectuals: Scission or Mimesis," originally published in Spanish in 1985. She argues there that the intellectual must regain a relative autonomy from politics, without being completely separate from it: "The romantic idea of the organic continuity between culture, ideology, and politics frequently produces undesirable associations, but the claim for a radical autonomy between these spheres hinders the grasping of the formal and conceptual complexity of their links. At the same time, it does not prevent political radicalization from subordinating culture or, in periods like the

one in which we are living now, culture from being endowed with regional fantasies of social independence" (259).

18. A similar sense of displacement of an older left intelligentsia seems to be involved in the decisions of many prominent left-wing Venezuelan intellectuals, such as Elisabeth Burgos or Teodoro Petkoff, to identify publicly with the opposition to Chávez, or of many writers and artists formerly associated with the Sandinistas to leave the party and join the electoral front organized by Sergio Ramírez. Similar cases could be found in most Latin American countries today.

19. See, e.g., Quijano, "Coloniality of Power, Eurocentrism, and Latin America."

20. Apropos the armed struggle, Sarlo notes in her column on Kirchner in *La Nación*: "Muchos sabemos por experiencia que se necesitaron años para romper con esas convicciones. No simplemente para dejarlas atrás o porque fueron derrotadas, sino porque significaron una equivocación." [Many of us know from experience that it took years to break away from these beliefs. Not simply to leave them behind or because they were defeated, but rather because they were a mistake.] I will take up this quote from Sarlo in particular, and more generally the question of what I call the paradigm of disillusion in the representation of the armed struggle, in chapter 6. Just to anticipate briefly that discussion here: the new Latin American Left, however pragmatically oriented it may be—and I am certainly not opposed to pragmatism—needs to recover what was positive in the heritage of the armed struggle and sixties radicalism, including the experience of the Chilean parliamentary "road to socialism," rather than simply renounce those experiences as a youthful "error."

21. See the classic study by Ardao, *Genesis de la idea y el nombre de América Latina*; and Mignolo, *The Idea of Latin America*.

22. Moraña offers a sharply etched, though not unsympathetic, portrait of the marea rosada in "La 'marea rosa' en América Latina o ¿qué queda de la izquierda?"

23. Saskia Sassen has been perhaps the most authoritative exponent of this idea. See her *Territory, Authority, Rights*.

24. In early twentieth-century Marxism, there was a nagging debate over whether a right-wing epistemology—the usual culprits were Kantianism or positivism—could coexist with left-wing politics. The question of Borges might be seen as the reverse of this: how does a left-wing or nominalist epistemology coexist with a right-wing or conservative politics? That is of course also a question about the nature of the literary baroque in both Spain and Latin America.

CHAPTER SIX: BEYOND THE PARADIGM OF DISILLUSION

This chapter is loosely based on "Rethinking the Armed Struggle in Latin America," *boundary 2*, 36.1 (spring 2009): 47–60.

1. Sarlo, "Kirchner actua como si fuera un soberano."

2. Apropos this issue in particular, there was an intense debate among Argentine intellectuals of the Left several years ago, triggered by an essay by the phi-

losopher Oscar del Barco, "No matarás," which dealt with the consequences of an ill-fated attempt to create a guerrilla *foco* in the province of Salta in 1964, in which two young recruits were executed by the guerrilla allegedly for treason (a similar incident is narrated in Che Guevara's *Reminiscences of the Cuban Revolutionary War*). Del Barco, a onetime supporter of the group involved (though apparently not himself a combatant), assumes moral responsibility for these killings, and argues that other intellectuals of the Argentine Left should do the same. Del Barco's text and the responses to it appear in Spanish in Belzagui, *Sobre la responsabilidad*.

3. For an earlier overview, written after the death of Che Guevara in 1967 but still infused with a sense of the possibility of victory, see Gott, *Guerrilla Movements in Latin America*. (Not incidentally, Gott's most recent book is a sympathetic portrait of Hugo Chávez.) A recent study of narratives of the armed struggle that explicitly seeks to avoid the paradigm of disillusion (without on the other hand defending or idealizing it as a strategy) is my colleague Juan Duchesne's new book, *La guerrilla narrada*.

4. Stoll, *Rigoberta Menchú and the Story of All Poor Guatemalans*, 282.

5. I owe this idea to Ignacio Sánchez Prado.

6. The narrative of the repentant guerrilla resembles what Alain Badiou calls, referring to the neoconservative conversion narratives of the New Philosophers in France, a "personal Thermidor," whose authority is founded precisely on the fact that one has been (or claims to have been) a leftist militant. See Badiou's essay "What Is a Thermidorean?," in *Metapolitics*, esp. 124. There are elements of this in Sarlo's position too. One of the things that is refreshing about the stories and novels of the late Roberto Bolaño is that he didn't buy into the paradigm of disillusion. His semiautobiographical (and sometimes neopicaresque) characters are, like himself, bohemians and leftists who have been defeated and have to make do, sometimes nihilistically or violently, in a world not of their choosing. But unlike the failed father figure at the end of *Amores perros*, they are not remorseful or repentant, and sometimes, they find ways to get revenge on their victimizers.

7. Some readers may recall that it was against such a "historicist" conception of history, then championed by the Left rather than, as today, by the Right, that Debray's own mentor, Louis Althusser, argued lucidly in now also largely forgotten books like *For Marx* or *Reading Capital*.

8. It is not irrelevant to note too the recent spread of armed struggle in rural areas of Nepal and some states of India, due to old rural class contradictions aggravated by the economic boom in the Indian subcontinent generated by neoliberal policies. The question of the relation of the peasantry and armed struggle both in the past and the present requires a more careful discussion than I can undertake here.

9. The relation between political militancy and modern Latin American literature, and then the severing of that relation, is the theme of Jean Franco's book, *The Decline and Fall of the Lettered City*.

10. One of the great anthologies of modern Latin American poetry was the collection of poems by writers killed or "disappeared" in the armed struggle, *Poesía trunca*, edited by Mario Benedetti.

11. Debray, "The Long March in Latin America."

12. Randall, *Sandino's Daughters*; also Rodríguez, *Women, Guerrillas, and Love*.

CHAPTER SEVEN: THE SUBALTERN AND THE STATE

A talk I presented at the Brown University Global Humanities Institute, June 1–3, 2009, is the basis for this chapter. My thanks to Tony Bogues for hosting me and to the participants—young scholars in the humanities drawn from the countries of the Global South—for whom these issues are more than academic ones. I should note that, based on his own experiences in the Manley government in Jamaica, Tony is skeptical about my argument here.

1. Rodríguez, "Between Cynicism and Despair."

2. Laclau, *On Populist Reason*, 261, n. 27. Laclau means to distinguish "becoming the state," an idea he takes from Gramsci, from "taking state power."

3. Rabasa, "Exception to the Political," in *Without History*, 251.

4. "Lo que la deconstrucción quiere es precisamente interrumpir la constitución de la hegemonía (que no es la del subalterno) en nombre de una política *distinta a* la relación hegemonía-subalternidad, construida con el único propósito de la subordinación" (Williams, "La desconstrucción y los estudios subalternos," 241).

5. Ranajit Guha himself goes to some lengths to distinguish hegemony and domination, famously characterizing British rule in India as "domination without hegemony" (Guha, *Dominance without Hegemony*).

6. Guha, "On Some Aspects of the Historiography of Colonial India," 35. Which is not to say of course that elements of defeated classes, or of elite classes in decomposition, such as the petty nobility in the transition from feudalism to capitalism, could not migrate in class or status terms to form part of the subaltern sectors of a given society.

7. This is essentially the argument of Michel-Rolph Trouillot's classic studies, *Haiti: State against Nation* and *Silencing the Past*.

8. I owe this idea to Juan Antonio Hernández, "Hacia una historia de lo imposible." The recent bibliography of the debate on this point is extensive, but see besides Trouillot, noted above, e.g., Fick, *The Making of Haiti*; Geggus, *Haitian Revolutionary Studies*; Dubois, *The Avengers of the New World*; Fischer, *Modernity Disavowed*; and Buck-Morss, *Hegel, Haiti, and Universal History*. Fischer notes the paradox that the idea of Haiti as an autonomous nation-state was initially directed *against* emancipation, in the sense that the slave owners wanted to become independent from France, which had (briefly) moved to abolish slavery after the revolution.

9. "[Machiavelli] revealed that what was needed, if Italian unity was to be

achieved, was for a nobody starting with nothing and from nowhere in particular, but outside the framework of an established State, to bring together the fragmented elements of a divided country, without any preconceived notion of unity which might have been formulated in terms of existing political concepts (all of which were bad)" (Althusser, *The Future Lasts Forever*, 220).

10. It would be useful to take up again in this regard the work of Poulantzas on the nature of the state: e.g., his *State, Power, Socialism*. For a thorough, although in some ways now dated overview, see Jessop, *Nicos Poulantzas*.

11. My friend Julio Ramos offers the following description of the situation in Venezuela today: "Creo que . . . [es] un error al pensar a Chávez como sinónimo del estado venezolano. A pesar del impulso centralizador del autoritarismo, legitimado por pactos populistas cada vez más frágiles, el estado venezolano es un estado muy dividido y disperso. Es una máquina incapaz de ejercer el monopolio sobre la violencia ni de controlar centralmente los flujos tan complejos del capital, administrado por nuevas manos mediadoras. De modo previsible, la saturación ideológica y discursiva funciona en parte como una zona de sutura del caos ideológico en el país. Y a la vez, la saturación ideológica, muy notable, tanto en los medios visuales como 'letrados' más tradicionales, es una gran *INDUSTRIA* de la opinión, una industria en el riñón mismo de los flujos de una aparatosa economía de servicio promovida por el estado. Creo que sería un error pensar la producción de la 'opinión' o de la cultura meramente como una zona de elaboración simbólica: es una zona que genera muchos, muchos, empleos" (I think it is an error to think of Chávez as synonymous with the Venezuelan state. In spite of the centralizing authoritarian impulse, legitimated by ever more fragile populist pacts, the Venezuelan state is a very divided and dispersed state. It is a machine incapable of exercising a monopoly on violence and of controlling centrally the complex flows of capital, administered by new mediators. In a way that could have been anticipated, the ideological and discursive saturation functions as a zone of suture for the ideological chaos of the country. And at the same time, this ideological saturation, notable as much in the audio-visual media as in the more traditional "lettered" public sphere, is a giant INDUSTRY of opinion, an industry at the center of the flows generated by the vaunted service economy promoted by the state. I think it would be an error to see the production of "opinion" or culture simply as a zone of symbolic elaboration: it is a zone that generates many, many jobs). Julio Ramos, personal communication, January 20, 2010. See also Fernandes, *Who Can Stop the Drums*.

12. Sassen, *Territory, Authority, Rights*, 419.

13. I'm not aware if the Zapatistas have made a self-criticism of their miscalculation; I suspect not. Rabasa makes the case for the Zapatista position in general in *Without History*, but does not take up in particular their decision to sit out the 2006 elections and its consequences, which, it seems to me at least, have been clearly negative. Barbara Epstein—speaking in a recent interview about the

links between the libertarian tendencies of the U.S. New Left and the rise of cultural studies, which also privileged an antistatist paradigm, puts the problem succinctly: "This anarchist streak made a certain amount of sense in that historical context [the sixties]. It was true that the liberals running the state were a large part of the problem. But I think that in the wake of the '60s, particularly in the '80s and '90s, the anarchist critique and the attack of the academic left on the liberal state has in fact strengthened the right. The project of the right has been to destroy the New Deal and the idea that the state has a responsibility for social welfare. Basically what you've had is the academic left backing that up. They're clearly not conservatives, but I do think that they have unwittingly colluded with and strengthened the right." Victor Cohen, "Interview with Barbara Epstein," 260.

14. Spivak, *Outside in the Teaching Machine*, 78.

15. García Linera, "State Crisis and Popular Power," 75.

16. See, e.g., Spivak's essay "Responsibility," in *Other Asias*, 58–96.

17. I invoke here the title of one of the canonic texts of Andean indigenous writing in the colonial period, Huamán Poma's *Primera corónica y buen gobierno*.

18. By "Schmittian" I refer to Derrida's sustained critique of Carl Schmitt's postulation of the friend/enemy distinction as constitutive of the political, which became paradigmatic in some ways for deconstructive approaches to politics: Derrida, *Politics of Friendship*. What I said earlier about the project to merge Latinamericanism and deconstruction could also be said of Derrida's critique of Schmitt: that it involves a rejection of politics as such. In Derrida's case, the critique leads to something like the advanced "liberalism" (in the best sense of the word) of "the democracy to come" (but apparently a democracy without political ideologies or parties); in the case of the antistatist or "posthegemonic" articulation of subalternism it leads to a kind of millenarian ultraleftism, which is also post-political. I will come back to this point at the end of this chapter. However, it may be worth remarking here that there is not as much distance between these alternatives as might appear: both are forms of what Hegel called "the beautiful soul."

19. Spivak, *Other Asias*, 245–46, 247.

20. García Linera, "El 'descubrimiento' del Estado" (2008), 75, translation by Bruno Bosteels. I am indebted to Bosteels for bringing this text to my attention in his very insightful discussion of García Linera in an as-yet unpublished essay, "The Leftist Hypothesis: Communism in the Age of Terror."

21. García Linera expressed this idea in his speech at the meeting of the Latin American Studies Association in Montreal in 2007. Rabasa offers a paraphrase as well as a fairly sharp critique of García Linera's speech, including this phrase, (and of the MAS project in general) in *Without History*, esp. 271–80.

Bibliography

Achúgar, Hugo. "Local/Global Latinamericanisms: 'Theoretical Babbling,' apropos Roberto Fernández Retamar." In *The Latin American Cultural Studies Reader*, edited by Ana del Sarto, Alicia Ríos, and Abril Trigo, 669–85. Durham: Duke University Press, 2004.

Adorno, Teodor. *Philosophy of Modern Music*. Translated by Anne Mitchell and Wesley Bomter. New York: Seabury, 1973.

Alonso, Carlos. *The Burden of Modernity: The Rhetoric of Cultural Discourse in Spanish America*. New York: Oxford University Press, 1998.

———. *The Spanish American Regional Novel: Modernity and Autochthony*. Cambridge: Cambridge University Press, 1990.

Althusser, Louis. *The Future Lasts Forever*. 1971; New York: New Press, 1993.

———. "Ideology and Ideological State Apparatuses." In *Lenin and Philosophy*, 127–88. New York: Monthly Review Press, 1971.

Anzaldúa, Gloria. *Borderlands: The New Mestiza — La Frontera*. San Francisco: Spinsters/Aunt Lute, 1987.

Ardao, Arturo. *Genesis de la idea y el nombre de América Latina*. Caracas: CELARG, 1993.

Aronna, Michael. *"Pueblos Enfermos": The Discourse of Illness in the Turn-of-the-Century Spanish and Latin American Essay*. Chapel Hill: University of North Carolina Press (North Carolina Studies in the Romance Languages and Literatures), 1999.

Avelar, Idelber. *The Letter of Violence: Essays on Narrative, Ethics, and Politics*. New York: Palgrave Macmillan, 2005.

———. *The Untimely Present: Postdictatorial Latin American Fiction and the Task of Mourning*. Durham: Duke University Press, 1999.

Badiou, Alain. *Metapolitics*. London: Verso, 2005.

Barragán, Rossana, and Silvia Rivera Cusicanqui, eds. *Debates post coloniales: Una introducción a los estudios de la subalternidad*. La Paz: Editorial historias-SEPHIS-Aruwiyiri, 1997.

Bauer, Otto. *The Question of Nationalities and Social Democracy*. Edited by Ephraim J. Nimni, translated by Joseph O'Donnell. 1907; Minneapolis: University of Minnesota Press, 2000.

Beasley-Murray, Jon. *Posthegemony: Political Theory and Latin America*. Minneapolis: University of Minnesota Press, 2011.

———, ed. *Towards a New Latin Americanism*. Special issue of *Journal of Latin American Cultural Studies* 11.3 (2002).

Bell, Daniel. *The Cultural Contradictions of Capitalism*. New York: Basic Books, 1976.

Belzagui, Pablo Reni. *Sobre la responsabilidad: No matar*. Córdoba: Ediciones del Cíclope/La Intemperie, 2007. A selection (in English) appeared in *Journal of Latin American Cultural Studies* 16.2 (2007): 111–82.

Benedetti, Mario. *Poesía trunca*. Havana: Casa de las Américas, 1977.

Bosteels, Bruno. "The Ethical Superstition." In *The Ethics of Latin American Literary Criticism*, edited by Erin Graff Zivin, 11–24. New York: Palgrave Macmillan, 2007.

———. "The Leftist Hypothesis: Communism in the Age of Terror." Unpublished manuscript, n.d.

Branche, Jerome. *Malungaje: hacia una poética de la diáspora africana*. Bogotá: Biblioteca Nacional/Ministerio de la Cultura, 2009.

Brown, Wendy. *State of Injury: Power and Freedom in Late Modernity*. Princeton: Princeton University Press, 1995.

Buck-Morss, Susan. *Hegel, Haiti, and Universal History*. Pittsburgh: University of Pittsburgh Press, 2009.

Castañeda, Jorge. "Latin America's Left Turn." *Foreign Affairs* 85 (May–June, 2006): 28–43.

———. "Morning in Latin America." *Foreign Affairs* 87 (September–October 2008): 126–39.

———. *Utopia Unarmed: The Latin American Left after the Cold War*. New York: Vintage, 1993.

Castillo, Alejandro, Federico Galende, Sergio Villalobos, and Alberto Moreiras. "Pantanillos ponzoñosos." *Revista de Crítica Cultural* 34 (2006): 78–87.

Castro-Goméz, Santiago, and Eduardo Mendieta, eds. *Teorías sin disciplina: Latinoamericanismo, postcolonialidad y globalización en debate*. Mexico: Porrua/Universidad San Francisco, 1998.

Chakrabarty, Dipesh. *Provincializing Europe: Postcolonial Thought and Historical Difference*. Princeton: Princeton University Press, 2000.

Chávez, Hugo. *La unidad latinoamericana*, edited by Sergio Rinaldi. Melbourne: Ocean Sur, 2006.

Cohen, Victor. "Interview with Barbara Epstein." *Works and Days* 55–56 (2010): 251–62.

Cornejo Polar, Antonio. "Mestizaje e hibridez: Los riesgos de las metáforas." *Revista Iberoamericana* 180 (July–September 1997): 341–44.

Davis, Richard Harding. *Soldiers of Fortune*. New York: American News Co., 1897.

Debray, Regis. *La crítica de las armas*. 2 vols. Mexico City: Siglo Veintiuno, 1975.

———. "The Long March in Latin America." *New Left Review* 1 (September–October 1965): 17–58.

———. *Revolution in the Revolution: Armed Struggle and Political Struggle in Latin America*. Translated by Bobbye Ortiz. New York: Grove Press, 1967.

de la Cadena, Marisol. *Indigenous Mestizos: The Politics of Race and Culture in Cuzco, Peru*. Durham: Duke University Press, 2000.

de la Campa, Román. *Latin Americanism*. Minneapolis: University of Minnesota Press, 1999.

del Sarto, Ana, Alicia Ríos, and Abril Trigo. *The Latin American Cultural Studies Reader*. Durham: Duke University Press, 2004.

del Valle Escalante, Emilio. *Maya Nationalisms and Postcolonial Challenges in Guatemala: Coloniality, Modernity, and Identity Politics*. Santa Fe: School of Advanced Research, 2009.

de Man, Paul. *Allegories of Reading*. New Haven: Yale University Press, 1979.

Derrida, Jacques. *Politics of Friendship*. London: Verso, 1997.

Dove, Patrick. *The Catastrophe of Modernity: Tragedy and the Nation in Latin American Literature*. Lewisburg, Penn.: Bucknell University Press, 2004.

Dubois, Laurent. *The Avengers of the New World: The Story of the Haitian Revolution*. Cambridge: Harvard University Press, 2004.

Duchesne, Juan. *La guerrilla narrada: Acción, acontecimiento, sujeto*. San Juan, Puerto Rico: Ediciones Callejón, 2010.

Fernandes, Sujatha. *Who Can Stop the Drum?: Urban Social Movements in Chávez's Venezuela*. Durham: Duke University Press, 2010.

Fick, Carolyn. *The Making of Haiti: The Saint Domingue Revolution from Below*. Knoxville: University of Tennessee Press, 1990.

Fischer, Sibylle. *Modernity Disavowed: Haiti and the Cultures of Slavery in the Age of Revolution*. Durham: Duke University Press, 2004.

Flores, Juan. *From Bomba to Hip-Hop: Puerto Rican Culture and Latino Identity*. New York: Columbia University Press, 2000.

Franco, Jean. *The Decline and Fall of the Lettered City: Latin America in the Cold War*. Cambridge: Harvard University Press, 2002.

García, Cristina. *Dreaming in Cuban*. New York: Ballantine, 1993.

García Canclini, Néstor. *Consumidores y ciudadanos*. Mexico City: Grijalbo, 1995.

———. *Hybrid Cultures*. Minneapolis: University of Minnesota Press, 1995.

García Linera, Álvaro. Address. Latin American Studies Association annual meeting, Montreal, Canada, September 5–7, 2007.

———. "El 'descubrimiento' del Estado." In *Las vías de la emancipación: Conversaciones con Álvaro García Linera*, edited by Pablo Stefanoni, Franklin Ramírez, and Maristella Svampa. Mexico City: Ocean Sur, 2008.

———. *Estado multinacional: Una propuesta democrática y pluralista para la extinción de la exclusión indígena*. La Paz: Editorial Malatesta, 2005.

———. "State Crisis and Popular Power." *New Left Review* 37 (January–February 2006): 73–85.

Geggus, David. *Haitian Revolutionary Studies*. Bloomington: Indiana University Press, 2002.

González Echevarría, Roberto. *Myth and Archive: A Theory of Latin American Narrative*. Durham: Duke University Press, 1998.

González Iñárritu, Alejandro, dir. *Amores perros* (film). Mexico City: Altavista, 2000.

Gott, Richard. *Guerrilla Movements in Latin America*. New York: Doubleday, 1971.

Graff Zivin, Erin, ed. *The Ethics of Latin American Literary Criticism*. New York: Palgrave Macmillan, 2007.

Guevara, Ernesto "Che." *Guerrilla Warfare*. New York: Monthly Review, 1961.

Guha, Ranajit. *Dominance without Hegemony: History and Power in Colonial India*. Cambridge: Harvard University Press, 1997.

———. *History at the Limit of World-History*. New York: Columbia University Press, 2002.

———. "On Some Aspects of the Historiography of Colonial India." In *Selected Subaltern Studies*, edited by Ranajit Guha and Gayatri Spivak, 37–44. New York: Oxford University Press, 1988.

———. "Preface." In *Selected Subaltern Studies*, edited by Ranajit Guha and Gayatri Spivak, 35–36. New York: Oxford University Press, 1988.

———. "Subaltern Studies: Projects for Our Time and Their Convergence." In *Latin American Subaltern Studies Reader*, edited by Ileana Rodríguez, 35–46. Durham: Duke University Press, 2001.

Hardt, Michael, and Antonio Negri. *Commonwealth*. Cambridge: Harvard University Press, 2009.

———. *Empire*. Cambridge: Harvard University Press, 2000.

———. *Multitude: War and Democracy in the Age of Empire*. New York: Penguin Press, 2004.

Hartmann, Geoffrey. "The Philomela Project." In *Minor Prophecies: The Literary Essay in the Culture Wars*, 164–75. Cambridge: Harvard University Press, 1991.

Harvey, David. *A Brief History of Neoliberalism*. Oxford: Oxford University Press, 2005.

Hegel, George W. F. *The Philosophy of History*. Version and translation by J. Sibree. New York: Dover, 1956.

Herlinghaus, Hermann. *Violence without Guilt: Ethical Narratives from the Global South*. New York: Palgrave Macmillan, 2008.

Hernández, Juan Antonio. "Hacia una historia de lo imposible: La revolución haitiana y el 'Libro de Pinturas' de José Antonio Aponte." Ph.D. dissertation, University of Pittsburgh, 2006.

Huntington, Samuel. *The Clash of Civilizations and the Remaking of the World Order*. New York: Simon and Schuster, 1996.

———. *Who Are We? The Challenges to America's National Identity*. New York: Simon and Schuster, 2004.

Jameson, Fredric. *The Geopolitical Aesthetic: Cinema and Space in the World System*. Bloomington: Indiana University Press, 1992.

———. *Postmodernism, or, The Cultural Logic of Late Capitalism*. Durham: Duke University Press, 1991.

Jenckes, Kate. "The 'New Latin Americanism,' and the End of Regionalist Thinking?" *New Centennial Review* 4.3 (2004): 247–70.

———. *Reading Borges after Benjamin: Allegory, Afterlife, and the Writing of History*. Albany: State University of New York Press, 2007.

Jessop, Bob. *Nicos Poulantzas: Marxist Theory and Political Strategy*. New York: St. Martin's Press, 1985.

Kerr, Lucille. "Academic Relations and Latin American Fictions." *Journal of Narrative Technique* 27.1 (1997): 25–53.

Kusch, Rodolfo. *Indigenous and Popular Thinking in América*. Translated by María Lugones and Joshua Price. Durham: Duke University Press, 2010.

Laclau, Ernesto. "Deriva populista y centroizquierda latinoamericana." At http://www.aporrea.org/, October 10, 2006.

———. *On Populist Reason*. London: Verso, 2007.

Larsen, Neil. "Latin-Americanism without Latin America: 'Theory' as a Surrogate Periphery in the Metropolitan University." *A Contra Corriente* 3.3 (Spring 2006): 37–46.

———. *Reading North by South*. Minneapolis: University of Minnesota Press, 1995.

Levinson, Brett. *The Ends of Literature: Latin American Literature in the Neoliberal Marketplace*. Stanford: Stanford University Press, 2001.

Lewis, Tom. "Latin Americanism and Imperialism after 9/11." *A Contra Corriente* 2.1 (Fall 2004): 1–20.

Mendieta, Eduardo. "Remapping Latin American Studies: Postcolonialism, Subaltern Studies, Post-Occidentalism, and Globalization Theory." In *Coloniality at Large: Latin America and the Postcolonial Debate*, edited by Mabel Moraña, Enrique Dussel, and Carlos Jáuregui, 286–306. Durham: Duke University Press, 2008.

Mészáros, István. "Bolívar and Chávez: The Spirit of Radical Determination." *Monthly Review* 59.3 (2007): 55–84.

Mignolo, Walter. "Coloniality of Power and Subalternity." In *The Latin American Subaltern Studies Reader*, edited by Ileana Rodríguez, 424–44. Durham: Duke University Press, 2001.

———. *The Idea of Latin America*. Malden, Mass.: Blackwell, 2005.

Morales, Mario Roberto. *La articulación de las diferencias, o el síndrome de Maximón: Los discursos literarios y políticos del debate interétnico en Guatemala*. Guatemala City: FLACSO, 1998. 2nd ed., Guatemala City: Consucultura, 2002.

Moraña, Mabel. "El *boom* del subalterno." *Revista de Crítica Cultural* 14 (1997): 48–53. Reprinted in *Debates críticos en América Latina: 36 números de la* Revista de Crítica Cultural *(1990–2008)*, vol. 2, edited by Nelly Richard, 101–10. Santiago, Chile: Arcis/Cuarto Propio, 2008.

———. "Borges y yo: Primera reflexión sobre 'El etnógrafo.'" In *Crítica impura*, 103–22. Madrid: Iberoamericana-Vervuert, 2004.

———. "La 'marea rosa' en América Latina o ¿qué queda de la izquierda?" In *Cultura y cambio social en América Latina*, edited by Mabel Moraña, 113–36. Frankfurt: Iberoamericana-Vervuert, 2008.

Moreiras, Alberto. *The Exhaustion of Difference: The Politics of Latin American Cultural Studies*. Durham: Duke University Press, 2001.

———. "Infrapolitics and the Thriller: A Prolegomenon to Every Possible Form of Antimoralist Literary Criticism: On Héctor Aguilar Camín's *La guerra de Galio* and *Morir en el golfo*." In *The Ethics of Latin American Literary Criticism*, edited by Erin Graff Zivin, 147–83. New York: Palgrave Macmillan, 2007.

———. "Irrupción y conservación en las Guerras Culturales." *Revista de Crítica Cultural* 17 (1998). Reprinted in *Debates críticos en América Latina: 36 números de la* Revista de Crítica Cultural *(1990–2008)*, vol. 2, edited by Nelly Richard, 123–30. Santiago, Chile: Arcis/Cuarto Propio, 2008.

———. *Línea de sombra: El no sujeto de lo político*. Santiago, Chile: Palinodia, 2006.

———. *Tercer espacio: Duelo y literatura en América Latina*. Santiago, Chile: ARCIS/Lom, 1999.

Negri, Antonio, and Giuseppe Cocco. *Global: Biopoder y luchas en una América Latina globalizada*. Buenos Aires: Paidos, 2006.

Nimni, Ephraim J. *Marxism and Nationalism: Theoretical Origins of a Political Crisis*. London: Pluto Press, 1994.

Portes, Alejandro, and Alex Stepick. *City on the Edge: The Transformation of Miami*. Berkeley: University of California Press, 1993.

Poulantzas, Nikos. *State, Power, Socialism*. London: New Left Books, 1978.

Quijano, Anibal. "Coloniality of Power, Eurocentrism, and Latin America." *Nepantla: Views from the South* 1–3 (2000): 533–80.

Rabasa, José. *Without History: Subaltern Studies, the Zapatista Insurgency, and the Specter of History*. Pittsburgh: University of Pittsburgh Press, 2010.

Rama, Ángel. *Transculturación narrativa en América Latina*. Mexico: Siglo Veintiuno, 1982.

Randall, Margaret. *Sandino's Daughters: Testimonies of Nicaraguan Women in Struggle*. New Brunswick: Rutgers University Press, 1994.

Reati, Fernando, and Gilberto Goméz Ocampo. "Académicos y *gringos malos*: La universidad norteamericana y la *barbarie cultural* en la novela latinoamericana reciente." *Revista Iberoamericana* 64 (1998): 184–85.

Reid, Michael. *Forgotten Continent: The Battle for Latin America's Soul*. New York: Yale University Press, 2008.

Richard, Nelly. "Cultural Peripheries: Latin America and Postmodernist Decentering." In *The Postmodernism Debate in Latin America*, edited by John Beverley, José Oviedo, and Michael Aronna, 217–22. Durham: Duke University Press, 1995.

————, ed. *Debates críticos en América Latina: 36 números de la* Revista de Crítica Cultural *(1990–2008)*, 2 vols. Santiago, Chile: Arcis/Cuarto Propio, 2008.

————. "Intersecting Latin America with Latin Americanism: Academic Knowledge, Theoretical Practice, and Cultural Criticism." In *The Latin American Cultural Studies Reader*, edited by Ana del Sarto, Alicia Ríos, and Abril Trigo, 643–54. Durham: Duke University Press, 2004.

Rodríguez, Ileana. "Between Cynicism and Despair: Constructing the Generic/ Specifying the Particular." In *New World (Dis)Orders and Peripheral Strains: Specifying Cultural Dimensions in Latin American and Latino Studies*, edited by Michael Piazza and Marc Zimmerman, 229–42. Chicago: Marcha/Abrazo Press, 1998.

————, ed. *Latin American Subaltern Studies Reader*. Durham: Duke University Press, 2001.

————. *Liberalism at Its Limits: Crime and Terror in the Latin American Cultural Text*. Pittsburgh: University of Pittsburgh Press, 2009.

————. *Women, Guerrillas, and Love: Understanding War in Central America*. Minneapolis: University of Minnesota Press, 1996.

Rojo, Grinor. *Las armas de las letras: Ensayos neoarielistas*. Santiago, Chile: LOM, 2008.

Sader, Emir. *The New Mole*. London: Verso, 2011.

Said, Edward. *Orientalism*. New York: Pantheon, 1979.

Saldívar, José David. *Border Matters: Remapping American Cultural Studies*. Berkeley: University of California Press, 1997.

————. *The Dialectics of Our America: Genealogy, Cultural Critique, and Literary History*. Durham: Duke University Press, 1991.

Santí, Enrico Mario. *Ciphers of History: Latin American Readings for a Cultural Age*. New York: Palgrave Macmillan, 2005.

Sarlo, Beatriz. "Contra la mimesis: Izquierda cultural, izquierda política." *Revista de Crítica Cultural* 20 (2000): 22–23.

―――. "Los estudios culturales en la encrucijada valorativa." *Revista de Crítica Cultural* 15 (1997): 32–38.

―――. "Intellectuals: Scission or Mimesis." 1985. English translation in *The Latin American Cultural Studies Reader*, edited by Ana del Sarto, Alicia Ríos, and Abril Trigo, 250–61. Durham: Duke University Press, 2004.

―――. "Kirchner actua como si fuera un soberano." *La Nación* (June 22, 2006). At www.lanacion.com.ar/.

―――. "Raymond Williams: Una relectura." In *Nuevas perspectivas sobre/desde América Latina: El desafío de los estudios culturales*, edited by Mabel Moraña, 309–18. Santiago, Chile: Cuarto Propio/IILI, 2000.

―――. *Tiempo pasado: Cultura de la memoria y giro subjetivo*. Buenos Aires: Siglo Veintiuno, 2005.

Sassen, Saskia. *Territory, Authority, Rights: From Medieval to Global Assemblages.* Princeton: Princeton University Press, 2006.

Sommer, Doris. *Foundational Fictions: The National Romances of Latin America.* Berkeley: University of California Press, 1991.

Spivak, Gayatri. *The Death of a Discipline.* New York: Columbia University Press, 2003.

―――. *Other Asias.* Malden, Mass.: Blackwell, 2008.

―――. *Outside in the Teaching Machine.* New York: Routledge, 1993.

Stoll, David. *Rigoberta Menchú and the Story of All Poor Guatemalans.* Boulder: Westview, 1999.

Taylor, Charles. "The Politics of Recognition." In *Multiculturalism: Examining the Politics of Recognition*, edited by Amy Gutman, 25–74. Princeton: Princeton University Press, 1994.

Trigo, Abril. "The 1990s: Practices and Polemics within Latin American Cultural Studies." In *The Latin American Cultural Studies Reader*, edited by Ana del Sarto, Alicia Ríos, and Abril Trigo, 347–74. Durham: Duke University Press, 2004.

Trouillot, Michel-Rolph. *Haiti: State against Nation.* New York: Monthly Review Press, 1990.

―――. *Silencing the Past: Power and the Production of History.* Boston: Beacon Press, 1995.

Virno, Paolo. "Virtuosity and Revolution: The Political Theory of Exodus." In *Radical Thought in Italy: A Potential Politics*, edited by Paolo Virno and Michael Hardt, 189–212. Minneapolis: University of Minnesota Press, 1996.

Volek, Emil, ed. *Latin America Writes Back: Postmodernity in the Periphery.* New York: Routledge, 2002.

Volpi, Jorge. *El fin de la locura.* Barcelona: Seix Barral, 2003.

―――. *El insomnio de Bolívar: Cuatro consideraciones sobre América Latina en el siglo XXI.* Barcelona: Random House Mondadori, 2009.

Williams, Gareth. "La desconstrucción y los estudios subalternos." In *Trienta años de estudios literarios/culturales latinoamericanistas en los Estados Unidos*, edited by Hernán Vidal. Pittsburgh: Instituto Internacional de Literatura Iberoamericana, 2008.

————. *The Other Side of the Popular: Neoliberalism and Subalternity in Latin America*. Durham: Duke University Press, 2002.

Yúdice, George, and Juan Flores. "Living Borders/Buscando América: Languages of Latino Self-Formation." *Social Text* 24 (1990): 57–84.

Žižek, Slavoj. "Multiculturalism, or The Cultural Logic of Multinational Capitalism." *New Left Review* 1.225 (September–October 1997): 28–51.

Index

Note: page numbers followed by "n" refer to endnotes.

Hardt, Michael: on Bauer, 131n6; on Bolivian social movements, 42; on Empire and multitude, 26–32, 41, 56–57, 101, 124–25; on hybridity, 38; nation-state and, 126

Hartmann, Geoffrey, 3, 44, 128n9

Hegel, G. W. F., 17, 19, 25, 37, 130n12, 143n18

hegemony: Gramsci on nation-state and, 38; Guha on domination vs., 141n5; Hardt & Negri's multitude and, 27–28, 31; Latin American nation-states and, 126; Moreiras on Bolivia and, 58; posthegemony, 56–57; state-subaltern relation and, 111–12; subalternity/hegemony distinction, 111–14

Herlinghaus, Hermann, 5

Hirsch, Marianne, 138n14

Hispanics. *See* Latinos/Hispanics (U.S.)

historicist narrative, 100–103, 140n7

Honduran coup, 66

La hora de los hornos (film), 105

humanities: neo-Arielism and, 20; neoconservative turn and, 73, 92; social sciences vs., 3, 47; Spivak on globalization and, 50; "studies" and, 69

Huntington, Samuel, 15–16, 18, 20, 25, 89, 125, 129n4

Hybrid Cultures (García Canclini), 132n8

hybridity, 38–39, 52–53, 76–78

I, Rigoberta Menchú (Menchú), 31, 61–62, 75, 76–77, 96, 98

identity politics: Brown's case against, 40; Hardt & Negri's multitude and, 27–32; Latinamericanism and, 4–5; and Left, reemergence of, 78; "lettered" creole-mestizo model, 106;

Mayan cultural nationalism and, 75–79; Moraña on, 80–83; multiculturalism and, 29; neoconservative turn and, 92; new social movements and, 106–7; radical multiculturalism and, 39–42; Sarlo on, 84–85; Spivak on "position without identity," 121–22

La ideología de la lucha armada (Morales), 137n5

"Ideology in General," 59

immigration, 15–16, 28

indigenous peoples: armed struggle and social movements, 107; Hardt & Negri's multitude and, 31–32; Mayan cultural nationalism and identity politics, 75–79; Mayan Holocaust, 76, 137n8; modernity and, 31

Inés de la Cruz, Sor Juana, 4

El insomnio de Bolívar (Volpi), 13–15, 66, 126

"Intellectuals: Scission or Mimesis" (Sarlo), 138n14

"interregnum," 45

Jameson, Fredric, 30, 38, 63, 74

Jenckes, Kate, 43, 132n3

Kadir, Djelal, 44, 134n11

Kautsky, Karl, 29

Kerr, Lucille, 135n1

Kirchner, Cristina, 87

Kirchner, Néstor, 87, 95–96, 139n20

Kissinger, Henry, 101

Kramer, Hilton, 74–75

Kristol, Irving, 137n3

Kusch, Rudolfo, 55

Laclau, Ernesto, 9, 52, 79, 81, 110, 134n9, 141n2

Larsen, Neil, 2

Machiavelli, Niccolò, 27, 141n9
magic realism, 38–39, 46, 132n9
Mallon, Florencia, 9
Marcuse, Herbert, 74
marea rosada ("pink tide"): "after 9/11" and, 7–15; armed struggle and, 95; commonalities, 7–8; Moraña on, 139n22; neoconservative turn and "alliance politics," 90–91; New Latin Americanism and, 45; posthegemony and the "people-state" and, 125; Sader on, 128n12; "studies" and solidarity with, 71; the subaltern and, 110–11; Volpi on, 14
Mariátegui, José Carlos, 31
Martí, José, 25, 67, 106
Marx, Karl, 28, 70
Marxism: Bauer's multinational state, 33–36; debate on right-wing epistemology and left-wing politics, 139n24; the "Indian question" and, 31, 107; Lenin on the "national question," 32–33; multiculturalism and, 27–28; subaltern studies and, 111
MAS (Movimiento al Socialismo), 10, 57–59, 118–23, 128n13
Maya Nationalisms and Postcolonial Challenges in Guatemala (del Valle), 138n9
Mayan cultural nationalism, 75–79
Mayan Holocaust, 76, 137n8
McOndo writers, 73
Menchú, Rigoberta, 31, 61–62, 75–77, 84–85, 96, 98, 133n6
Mendieta, Eduardo, 2, 135n4
mestizaje: adaptation of "the people" narrative, 38; discourse of, 78, 130n13; García Linera on ideal of, 119, 120; "Mestizaje e hibridez" (Cornejo Polar), 134n12, 135n4; "mestizaje intercultural," 77–79, 83

Mexico: as Latin American or North American, 129n4; PAN and PRI, 116–17; Zapatistas and PRD, 116–18, 142n13
Mignolo, Walter, 2, 58, 80, 131n3
minorities, Bauer on nation and, 34. *See also* multiculturalism
modernity: Chakrabarty on *adda* and, 49; communicative rationality and, 62; García Canclini on, 132n8; indigenous peoples and, 31; Mignolo on subaltern studies and, 131n3; Moraña on difference and, 81; Moreiras on difference and, 47; nation and, 32–39; socialism vs. capitalism and, 22–23; social movements and, 111; "studies" and, 69; tradition/modernity binary, 38
Molloy, Sylvia, 44
Morales, Mario Roberto: *La articulación de las diferencias*, 72, 75–79, 87–90, 93–94, 137n4; *La ideología de la lucha armada*, 137n5; *Los que se fueron por la libre*, 137n6
Morales Ayma, Evo, 57–59
Moraña, Mabel: "El boom del subalterno," 19, 63, 79, 138n10; "Borges y yo," 72, 79–83, 87–90, 93–94; on marea rosada, 139n22
Moreiras, Alberto: on Cornejo Polar, 134n12; "critical regionalism," 78; Galician nationalism and, 134n13; on "Latinamericanism" as term, 1, 127n3; *Línea de sombra*, 57–59, 132n1, 134n13, 135n17; neo-Arielism and, 19; *Tercer espacio*, 46–47. *See also The Exhaustion of Difference* (Moreiras)
Moretti, Franco, 50
The Motorcycle Diaries (Salles; film), 99

forms of, 103–4; waning of socialist bloc, 103

social movements and the state. *See* the subaltern and the state, relation between

Soderbergh, Steven, 99

Soldiers of Fortune (Davis), 64–66

solidarity or sympathy: first-wave deconstruction and, 3; Latinamericanism and, 3–4, 128n8; neoconservative turn and denial of, 90–91; Santí on, 133n4; Sarlo on, 84–85; "studies" and, 69; with "studies" vs. regional or national interests, 70–71

Sommer, Doris, 44, 65

South Africa, 104

Soviet Union, 8, 33, 103–4

Spinoza, Baruch, 26

Spivak, Gayatri, 10, 48, 50, 83, 117–23

Stalin, Joseph, 33–34

the state: "becoming the state" (Laclau), 9, 110; "bringing the state back in," 9–10; loss of confidence in, 111; neoconservatism and, 137n2; the "people-state," 125; the postsubaltern and, 8–9; sovereignty and state power, 114; Spivak on "reinventing," 121. *See also* the nation-state and nationalism; the subaltern and the state, relation between

"State Crisis and Popular Power" (García Linera), 117–23

State of Injury (Brown), 40, 132n11

Stepik, Alex, 16

Stoll, David, 61–63, 75, 77, 84–85, 98, 133n6

strategic essentialism, 52

Strauss, Leo, 73

Stravinsky, Igor, 74

"studies": argument *from* Latin America against, components of, 62–63; Davis's *Soldiers of Fortune* and, 66; neo-Arielist critique of, 62–63, 66–71; solidarity with regional and national interests vs., 70–71

the subaltern and subaltern studies: Chakrabarty on, 36; counter-collectivity, 122; deconstruction and, 46; dependency theory and, 131n3; Guha's definition of, 27; Hardt and Negri's multitude and, 26–27; identity politics, radical multiculturalism, and, 39–42; Latinamericanism articulated "from," 23–24; literary criticism and subaltern "otherness," 79–83; nation and, 36–38; neoconservative turn and, 87–88, 93–94; posthegemony and, 56; postsubalternism, 8–9, 111; radical heterogeneity of, 37, 39; "studies" and, 63; testimonial voice and, 62

the subaltern and the state, relation between: overview, 110–11; globalization and, 114–15; hegemony/subalternity distinction, 111–14; informal political subjects and, 115; neoconservative and ultraleftist alternatives, 123–26; social movements and state power, 114; Spivak vs. García Linera on, 118–23; transformative possibility, 115–16; Zapatista case, 116–18

the sublime, 53

sympathy. *See* solidarity or sympathy

Taylor, Charles, 61, 82

TCK (third or trans-culture kid), 136n9

Teorías sin disciplina (Castro-Goméz & Mendieta), 135n4

JOHN BEVERLEY is Distinguished Professor of Hispanic languages and literatures at the University of Pittsburgh. His books include *Aspects of Góngora's "Soledades"*; *Del Lazarillo al sandinismo: Estudios sobre la función ideológica de la literatura española e hispanoamericana*; *Literature and Politics in the Central American Revolutions* with Marc Zimmermann; *Against Literature*; *Subalternity and Representation*; and *Testimonio: On the Politics of Truth*. He has co-edited a number of books, including *The Postmodernism Debate in Latin America* with Michael Aronna and José Oviedo and *Texto y sociedad: Problemas de historia literaria* with Bridget Aldaraca and Edward Baker. He was a founding member of the Latin American Subaltern Studies group, and is a member of the editorial collective of the journal *boundary 2*. He co-edits the University of Pittsburgh Press book series Illuminations: Cultural Formations of the Americas, and is associate director of publications of the Instituto Internacional de Literatura Iberoamericana.

Library of Congress Cataloging-in-Publication Data
Beverley, John, 1943–
Latinamericanism after 9/11 / John Beverley.
p. cm.
Includes bibliographical references and index.
ISBN 978-0-8223-5100-9 (cloth : alk. paper)
ISBN 978-0-8223-5114-6 (pbk. : alk. paper)
1. Latin America—Study and teaching (Higher) 2. Latin America—History—1980–
3. Latin America—Politics and government—1980– I. Title.
Series: Post-Contemporary Interventions book series.
F1409.9.B48 2011
980.04072—dc22
2011010746